THE BRAHMĀ'S NET SUTRA

BDK English Tripiṭaka Series

THE BRAHMĀ'S NET SUTRA

(Taishō Volume 24, Number 1484)

Translated by

A. Charles Muller

and

Kenneth K. Tanaka

BDK America, Inc.
2017

First Printing, 2017
ISBN: 978-1-886439-65-8
Library of Congress Catalog Card Number: 2017949840

Published by
BDK America, Inc.
1675 School Street
Moraga, California 94556

Printed in the United States of America

A Message on the Publication of the English Tripiṭaka

The Buddhist canon is said to contain eighty-four thousand different teachings. I believe that this is because the Buddha's basic approach was to prescribe a different treatment for every spiritual ailment, much as a doctor prescribes a different medicine for every medical ailment. Thus his teachings were always appropriate for the particular suffering individual and for the time at which the teaching was given, and over the ages not one of his prescriptions has failed to relieve the suffering to which it was addressed.

Ever since the Buddha's Great Demise over twenty-five hundred years ago, his message of wisdom and compassion has spread throughout the world. Yet no one has ever attempted to translate the entire Buddhist canon into English throughout the history of Japan. It is my greatest wish to see this done and to make the translations available to the many English-speaking people who have never had the opportunity to learn about the Buddha's teachings.

Of course, it would be impossible to translate all of the Buddha's eighty-four thousand teachings in a few years. I have, therefore, had one hundred thirty-nine of the scriptural texts in the prodigious Taishō edition of the Chinese Buddhist canon selected for inclusion in the First Series of this translation project.

It is in the nature of this undertaking that the results are bound to be criticized. Nonetheless, I am convinced that unless someone takes it upon himself or herself to initiate this project, it will never be done. At the same time, I hope that an improved, revised edition will appear in the future.

It is most gratifying that, thanks to the efforts of more than a hundred Buddhist scholars from the East and the West, this monumental project has finally gotten off the ground. May the rays of the Wisdom of the Compassionate One reach each and every person in the world.

NUMATA Yehan
Founder of the English
Tripiṭaka Project

August 7, 1991

Editorial Foreword

In the long history of Buddhist transmission throughout East Asia, translations of Buddhist texts were often carried out as national projects supported and funded by emperors and political leaders. The BDK English Tripiṭaka project, on the other hand, began as a result of the dream and commitment of one man. In January 1982 Dr. NUMATA Yehan, founder of Bukkyō Dendō Kyōkai (Society for the Promotion of Buddhism), initiated the monumental task of translating the complete Taishō shinshū daizōkyō edition of the Chinese Tripiṭaka (Buddhist canon) into the English language. Under his leadership, a special preparatory committee was organized in April 1982. By July of the same year the Translation Committee of the English Tripiṭaka was officially convened.

The initial Committee included the following members: (late) HANAYAMA Shōyū (Chairperson), (late) BANDŌ Shōjun, ISHIGAMI Zennō, (late) KAMATA Shigeo, (late) KANAOKA Shūyū, MAYEDA Sengaku, NARA Yasuaki, (late) SAYEKI Shinkō, (late) SHIOIRI Ryōtatsu, TAMARU Noriyoshi, (late) TAMURA Kwansei, (late) URYŪZU Ryūshin, and YUYAMA Akira. Assistant members of the Committee were as follows: KANAZAWA Atsushi, WATANABE Shōgo, Rolf Giebel of New Zealand, and Rudy Smet of Belgium.

After holding planning meetings on a monthly basis, the Committee selected one hundred and thirty-nine texts for the First Series of the project, estimated to be one hundred printed volumes in all. The texts selected were not limited to those originally written in India but also included works composed in China and Japan. While the publication of the First Series proceeds, the texts for the Second Series will be selected from among the remaining works; this process will continue until all the texts, in Japanese as well as in Chinese, have been published. Given the huge scope of this project, accomplishing the English translations of all the Chinese and Japanese texts in the Taishō canon may take as long as one hundred years or more. Nevertheless, as Dr. NUMATA wished, it is the sincere hope of the Committee that this project will continue until completion, even after all the present members have passed away.

Dr. NUMATA passed away on May 5, 1994, at the age of ninety-seven. He entrusted his son, Mr. NUMATA Toshihide with the continuation and completion of the English Tripiṭaka project. Mr. Numata served for twenty-three years, leading the project forward with enormous progress before his sudden passing on February 16, 2017, at the age of eighty-four. The Committee previously lost its able and devoted first Chairperson, Professor HANAYAMA Shōyū, on June 16, 1995, at the age of sixty-three. In October 1995 the Committee elected Professor MAYEDA Sengaku (then Vice President of Musashino Women's College) as Chairperson, and upon the retirement of Professor Mayeda in July 2016, the torch was passed to me to serve as the third Chairperson. Despite these losses and changes we, the Editorial Committee members, have renewed our determination to carry out the noble ideals set by Dr. NUMATA. Present members of the Committee are Kenneth K. Tanaka (Chairperson), MAYEDA Sengaku, ICHISHIMA Shōshin, ISHIGAMI Zennō, KATSURA Shōryū, NARA Yasuaki, SAITŌ Akira, SHIMODA Masahiro, WATANABE Shōgo, and YONEZAWA Yoshiyasu.

The Numata Center for Buddhist Translation and Research was established in November 1984, in Berkeley, California, U.S.A., to assist in the publication of the translated texts. The Publication Committee was organized at the Numata Center in December 1991. In 2010, the Numata Center's operations were merged with Bukkyō Dendō Kyōkai America, Inc. (BDK America), and BDK America continues to oversee the publication side of the English Tripiṭaka project in close cooperation with the Editorial Committee in Tokyo.

At the time of this writing, in February 2017, the project has completed about sixty percent of the seven thousand one hundred and eighty-five Taishō pages of texts selected for the First Series. Much work still lies ahead of us but we are committed to the completion of the remaining texts in order to realize the grand vision of Dr. Numata, shared by Mr. Numata and Professor Hanayama, to make the Buddhist canon more readily accessible to the English-speaking world.

Kenneth K. Tanaka
Chairperson
Editorial Committee of
the BDK English Tripiṭaka

Publisher's Foreword

On behalf of the members of the Publication Committee, I am happy to present this volume as the latest contribution to the BDK English Tripiṭaka Series. The Publication Committee members have worked to ensure that this volume, as all other volumes in the series, has gone through a rigorous process of editorial efforts.

The initial translation and editing of the Buddhist scriptures found in this and other BDK English Tripiṭaka volumes are performed under the direction of the Editorial Committee in Tokyo, Japan. Both the Editorial Committee in Tokyo and the Publication Committee, headquartered in Moraga, California, are dedicated to the production of accurate and readable English translations of the Buddhist canon. In doing so, the members of both committees and associated staff work to honor the deep faith, spirit, and concern of the late Reverend Dr. Yehan Numata, who founded the BDK English Tripiṭaka Series in order to disseminate the Buddhist teachings throughout the world.

The long-term goal of our project is the translation and publication of the texts in the one hundred-volume Taishō edition of the Chinese Buddhist canon, along with a number of influential extracanonical Japanese Buddhist texts. The list of texts selected for the First Series of this translation project may be found at the end of each volume in the series.

As Chair of the Publication Committee, I am deeply honored to serve as the fifth person in a post previously held by leading figures in the field of Buddhist studies, most recently by my predecessor, John R. McRae.

In conclusion, I wish to thank the members of the Publication Committee for their dedicated and expert work undertaken in the course of preparing this volume for publication: Managing Editor Marianne Dresser, Dr. Hudaya Kandahjaya, Dr. Carl Bielefeldt, Dr. Robert Sharf, and Rev. Brian Kensho Nagata, Director of the BDK English Tripiṭaka Project.

A. Charles Muller
Chairperson
Publication Committee

Contents

Contents

Translators' Introduction

Origins of the Sutra: Its Structure and Content

The *Brahmā's Net Sutra* (Ch. *Fanwang jing,* Taishō 1484), a relatively short work of only two fascicles, plays an important niche role in the development of East Asian Mahayana Buddhism: it is the primary extant vinaya text that articulates a set of precepts from a Mahayana perspective, which takes its main audience to be "bodhisattva practitioners," mainly householders who remain engaged with society rather than becoming renunciant monks or nuns. Before the appearance of this text the monastic rules and regulations in East Asian Buddhism were defined fully by the "Hinayana" vinaya, most importantly the *Four-part Vinaya* (*Sifen lü,* Taishō 1428) associated with the Dharmaguptaka school in India. Once the *Brahmā's Net Sutra* made its appearance, the practices of the precepts in many East Asian schools diversified and certain groups of practitioners took up one or the other set of precepts, often utilizing both.

The study of vinaya materials is of great importance in Buddhist studies, and not simply because these works define the code of behavior for monks, nuns, and laypeople. They also provide, in a way seen in almost no other genre in the Buddhist canon, a snapshot of the historical realities of society in given periods of Buddhist history, especially revealing how Buddhist practitioners, both lay and monastic, interacted with their societies. The vinayas, and especially the discourse seen in this sutra, show monastic and lay Buddhist practitioners engaged at every level of society, from top to bottom. Buddhist practitioners were involved in military affairs, political intrigues, matchmaking, and every other sort of "mundane" social activity. The vinaya texts reveal how the Buddhist community in a certain age judged and dealt with such matters.

Presenting the *Brahmā's Net Sutra* solely as a vinaya work, however, continues an imbalanced view of the sutra that has been repeated since at least the Sui dynasty (581–618 C.E.). In fact only the second half of the sutra is a vinaya text.

The *Brahmā's Net Sutra* was written in two fascicles, each radically different in structure, content, theme, grammar, etc., from the other. Because of the extent of these differences many modern scholars consider that the two fascicles were originally two separate works.[1] The first fascicle discusses the forty Mahayana stages: the ten departures toward the destination, the ten nourishing mental states, the ten adamantine mental states, and the ten bodhisattva grounds. This fascicle is written in a markedly rough, largely ungrammatical quality of classical Chinese prose that is almost impenetrable in certain places. In fact, if not for the commentary by Daehyeon, on which we relied extensively in the process of preparing this translation, many sections may have been adjudged as being wholly unintelligible.

Regarding the significance of the *Brahmā's Net Sutra* among the apocryphal texts that deal with the forty stages, other texts compiled during roughly the same era, such as the *Pusa yingluo benye jing* (Taishō 1485), included better-organized and more comprehensive discussions of these stages. We can assume that the combination of the difficulty of the first fascicle and the availability of better articulations of the forty stages elsewhere, along with the fact that the Buddhist sangha was mostly far more interested in the precepts section, led to the first fascicle of the *Brahmā's Net Sutra* being largely ignored by both classical commentators and modern scholars. The most important East Asian classical commentators, including such major scholiasts as Zhiyi (538–597), in the *Tiantai pusajie shu* (Taishō 1812) and the *Pusajie yishu* (Taishō 1811) coauthored with Zhanding; Wonhyo (617–686), in the *Beommanggyeong bosal gyebon sagi* (*Hanguk bulgyo jeonseo* [*Collected Works of Korean Buddhism*] 1.586–604); and Fazang (643–712), in the *Fanwangjing pusa jieben shu* (Taishō 1813), ignored the first fascicle and commented only on the second. Modern translations and studies of the sutra also invariably leave out the first fascicle, usually not even mentioning its existence. The lone notable exception is the full commentary on the text by the Silla scholiast Daehyeon mentioned above, the *Beommanggyeong gojeokgi* (Taishō 1815).[2]

The second fascicle of the *Brahmā's Net Sutra* explains the ten grave precepts and the forty-eight minor precepts. These came to be referred to as the "bodhisattva precepts," the "great *Brahmā's Net* precepts," the "buddha precepts," and so forth. The second fascicle has been especially esteemed, studied, and circulated separately for more than a millennium as the scriptural authority for the Mahayana bodhisattva precepts, under such titles as the *Bodhisattva Vinaya Sutra,* the *Bodhisattva Prātimokṣa,* the *Brahmā's Net Prātimokṣa,* and so forth. Circulated as a separate text with these titles and commented on hundreds of times, it became the major textual source for the Mahayana vinaya and was very popular and influential in East Asia.

While the *Brahmā's Net Sutra* is known by various titles, the one given in the Taishō Shinshū Daizōkyō (derived from the title in the Goryeo Tripiṭaka) is *Brahmā's Net Sutra: The Mind-ground Dharma Gate Taught by Vairocana Buddha, Chapter Ten, in Two Fascicles.* The canonical story behind this sutra is that it was originally a massive work of one hundred and twenty fascicles, of which the Trepiṭaka Kumārajīva at the very end separately translated only the tenth chapter, the "Chapter on the Dharma Gate of the Bodhisattva's Stages of Practice." According to modern research, however, this text is not considered to be a translation by Kumārajīva of a chapter from a larger text but instead a work composed in China around 420, based on various Mahayana and Hinayana vinaya writings available at that time and including extensive discussion of indigenous Chinese moral concepts such as filial piety, etc. Some scholars believe that while traditional Chinese moral thought can be seen in the text, it is nonetheless originally an Indian text that was transmitted to China and further emended there. Whatever positions one might hold in this debate, there is no doubt that the text is based in the same matrix as the mainstream Mahayana thought of the *Flower Ornament Sutra* (*Huayan jing,* Taishō 278), the *Nirvana Sutra* (*Niepan jing,* Taishō 374), and the *Sutra for Humane Kings* (*Renwang jing,* Taishō 245). In fact, the extent to which the *Brahmā's Net Sutra* is in agreement with the *Huayan jing* is so pronounced that it is even regarded as the "concluding sutra" of the *Flower Ornament Sutra.*

The authority of the Mahayana precepts came to be widely accepted in China, Korea, and Japan. Especially in Japan, Saichō (767–822) used the *Brahmā's Net* precepts to integrate the vinaya trends at the time when Mahayana and Hinayana precepts were being used concurrently, and took these as the scriptural basis for the notion of a person who would practice the perfect and sudden precepts as a way of becoming a "Mahayana *bhikṣu.*"

In China, de facto Tiantai founder Zhiyi wrote the two-fascicle *Pusajie yishu* as a commentary on the *Brahmā's Net* precepts, drawing much attention to the text. Later Fazang, in composing his six-fascicle *Fanwangjing pusa jieben shu,* led the way for a proliferation of commentaries on the text. From these kinds of initial studies, this text did not merely eclipse the canonical vinayas that had preceded it but broadly embraced and reflected the conditions and demands of the society and sangha of the age. The *Brahmā's Net Sutra* thus became a finely tuned canonical resource and the primary authority for the Mahayana moral code.

Based on this text's far-reaching influence, research on the Hinayana canon began to decline in importance from the time of the Tang dynasty (618–907) in China; in Silla, from the time of unification (668), interest in Hinayana texts also began to fade. On the other hand, with the *Brahmā's Net* precepts as a basis, the Mahayana bodhisattva precepts took center stage as a subject of research and foundation for practice. In addition, the *Brahmā's Net Sutra* attracted considerable attention from scholars in Silla from schools other than the Vinaya tradition, who conducted their own extensive studies and published various commentaries, tables, indices, and extracts of the text.

The Development of the Mahayana Vinaya

The Mahayana vinaya came to the fore as an alternative to the Hinayana vinaya, most importantly the *Four-part Vinaya* of the Dharmaguptaka school, which had served as the basic framework for the vinaya for most East Asian schools up to that point. The emphasis in the *Brahmā's Net Sutra* turns to the development of a set of rules applicable for householders, providing guidelines for their modes of interaction with society in a more realistic way, which the monastically oriented set of rules in the old vinaya did not provide. The old vinaya had just five principles for laypeople; the Mahayana vinaya provided ten grave precepts and forty-eight minor precepts.

As compared with the ten basic Hinayana precepts for monks and nuns, the ten grave Mahayana precepts tend to focus more on the intentionality of the act (such as killing, stealing, lying, etc.), or the doer's enjoyment of the act, rather than the mere commission of the act itself. The precept regarding alcohol is concerned with its sale rather than its consumption. The precept against debauchery is defined to a great extent from the perspective of the degree to which one is taking advantage of another person through holding a position of greater power and so forth, rather than mere sexual indulgence. The precept regarding stealing discusses complicated issues of ownership, since the precept deals not only with monks but also with laypeople, who as part of everyday society must own and handle various kinds of property in various ways.

There is also a major new transition in regard to the reception of the precepts. While the ordination ceremony for the Hinayana precepts is clearly set and requires a specific number of officiants and witnesses, the Mahayana precepts, in order to address a situation in which there may be no or limited access to a qualified preceptor, can be obtained through the practitioner's having a vision of the Buddha in the process of extended periods of repentance. Various lengths of time are allowed for a layperson to obtain this requisite vision, with optional means provided in the event of a lack of success in obtaining it.[3] The forty-eight minor precepts have the flavor of ad hoc determinations dealing with various situations in the relations between monks, laypeople/donors, and the ruling class.

In the sutra itself, neither the ten grave precepts nor the forty-eight precepts have actual designatory labels attached. Thus, lists of labels or names for the ten and forty-eight precepts have traditionally been adopted from one of the major commentaries on the sutra. We have followed suit here and have adapted the section labels prepared by Daehyeon in his commentary, since his system of labels has been traditionally regarded as providing the most precise characterizations of the contents of each section.

THE BRAHMĀ'S NET SUTRA

Fascicle One

Exposition of the
Brahmā's Net Sutra

[Preface]

The doctrinal roots of our tradition are profound and the principle is not easily fathomed—therefore we subtly investigate the realm of the abstruse source. The myriad practices arise from the abode of deep faith—therefore the Indian Dharma master Kumārajīva recited and memorized this chapter, regarding it as the apex of the mind. This scripture originally consisted of one-hundred and twenty scrolls in sixty-one chapters. When Kumārajīva first entered the Great Method he harmonized the heterodoxy at Kapilavastu. In the third year of Hong Shi (402) the genuine wind was fanned in the east, and the Qin ruler Yao Xing enlightened all the kings to their profound mind of the great Dharma.

At Caotang Temple three thousand scholars worked together with Kumāra-jīva, translating more than fifty Hinayana and Mahayana texts, leaving the *Brahmā's Net Sutra* to be recited last. At that time [Dao]rong and [Dao]ying, along with three hundred others, simultaneously received the ten bodhisattva precepts. How could such benefits have been limited to that moment in time? Instead they were transmitted for many eons to come. Therefore, together with Daorong [Kumārajīva] separately published this mind-ground chapter. At that time more than three hundred people chanted this single chapter, and for this reason this book, arranged into eighty-one sections, was transmitted to later generations for memorization, recitation, and mutual instruction. It was entrusted to later scholars, noble people who loved the Way, with the wish that the *Brahmā's Net Sutra* would not disappear in future ages, when people will share in the vision of the dragon-flower.[4]

Preface to the *Brahmā's Net Sutra*
by Śramaṇa Sengzhao

The *Brahmā's Net Sutra* is truly the profound doctrinal source for the myriad teachings, providing the essential points for all the sutras. It provides the true

3

framework for the Great Sage to enlighten beings, the correct path for practitioners to climb the stairway. Therefore, even though the expedient lessons of the Tathā-gata are beyond measure, of the main themes [of Mahayana discourse] there are none that do not take guidance from the instructions in this sutra. Therefore, the Qin ruler, in order to enlighten all those within the kingdom, focused attention on scattered superficialities. Even though the text authoritatively discourses on all matters within the four seas, its main theme is the deeply profound.

Even if a gale were to overwhelm the eight borders of the kingdom, one may quiet one's mind beyond the world. Therefore, in the third year of Hong Shi, a strong wind fanned the East. At that time [the Qin emperor] invited the Indian Dharma master Kumārajīva to stay at Caodong Temple in Chang'an. Together with more than three thousand monks with proper academic training, he held the Sanskrit texts in his hand, dictated his translation and explication, and completed more than fifty works. All that remained was the *Brahmā's Net Sutra* in one hundred and twenty rolls and sixty-one chapters. Among these chapters, the tenth chapter, "On the Mind-ground of the Bodhisattvas," focused on articulating the stages of bodhisattva practice.

997b

At that time, Daorong and Daoying, along with three hundred or so others, received the bodhisattva precepts. Each of them recited this chapter, regarding it as the apex of the mind. The purposes of teacher and students were unified; [the monks] respectfully copied down this single chapter in eighty-one sections and spread it throughout the world in the hope of causing people to treasure *bodhi*. Since this is pursued by awakening to the principle, they wished for those in later generations to hear [this sutra,] as they had.

The Forty Stages

[Convocation]

Śākyamuni Buddha, residing in the state of the fourth concentration (*dhyāna*) in the royal palace of Maheśvara, together with innumerable Brahmā kings and inexplicable, untold multitudes of bodhisattvas, expounded the chapter of the Dharma gate of the mind-ground as explained by Vairocana Buddha in the world of the lotus flower platform store.

At that time the body of Śākyamuni emitted the radiance of wisdom, which illuminated from the heavenly palaces to the worlds of the lotus flower platform store. All the sentient beings in all of the worlds, seeing each other, were overcome with joy, but as they were unable to know the causes and conditions of this illumination, they all had thoughts of doubt. Countless celestial beings also gave rise to doubt.

Then, from within the assembly, the bodhisattva Mysterious Penetration Flower Radiance King arose from the *samādhi* of great brilliant flower radiance and, through the buddhas' supernormal power, emitted an adamantine white cloud-colored light that illuminated all the worlds. All the bodhisattvas from these worlds gathered at the assembly, and with a single mind [but speaking with] different mouths, they asked, "What are the characteristics of these lights?"

Śākyamuni then lifted the great assembly from this world, returning to the world of the lotus flower platform store, where amid a palace with hundreds of billions of rays of red-tinged adamant they saw Vairocana Buddha. A million lotus flowers vividly shone from above his seat.

Then Śākyamuni and the members of the great assembly simultaneously bowed in reverence at the feet of Vairocana Buddha. Śākyamuni said:

> By what causes and conditions can all of the sentient beings who live in the land and the air in this world achieve completion of the bodhisattva's path of the ten grounds? What are the characteristics of the attainment of buddhahood in the future?

This is as in the "Chapter on the Original Source of Buddha-nature," which extensively inquires about the seeds of all bodhisattvas.   997c

At that time Vairocana Buddha, greatly elated, manifested the *samādhi* of space-penetrating illumination of the eternally abiding Dharma body, which is the essential nature and original source of becoming a buddha, displaying it to the great multitude.

> Sons of the Buddha, listen carefully, think and practice well. I have cultivated the mind-ground for the duration of one hundred incalculably long eons (*kalpas*) in the past. With this as cause, I first cast off mundane folly and achieved perfect enlightenment under the name of Rocana. I dwelled in the Lotus Flower Platform Store World Ocean, which was surrounded by a thousand leaves, each leaf holding one world, which became a thousand worlds. I transformed these into a thousand Śākyas

overseeing a thousand worlds. As a consequence, each leaf-world further contained ten billion Mount Sumerus, ten billion suns and moons, ten billion of the four continents, ten billion Jambudvīpas, and ten billion bodhisattva Śākyas, sitting beneath ten billion *bodhi* trees, each expounding the bodhisattva mind-ground about which you have raised a question. The other nine hundred and ninety-nine Śākyas each manifested ten trillion Śākyas in the same way. Each of these thousand buddhas sitting atop the flowers was one of my transformation bodies. Each of the ten trillion Śākyas was one thousand Śākya transformation bodies. I am the source of all of these, and my name is Rocana Buddha.

At this moment, while seated on the lotus-store platform, Vairocana answered in detail the questions of the thousand Śākyas and ten trillion Śākyas in the form of the "Chapter on the Mind-ground Dharma."

Ten Departures toward the Destination

All buddhas should know that within the patience of firm faith there are ten entries and fruitions of the departures toward the destination. These are the mental states of (1) detachment, (2) morality, (3) tolerance, (4) zeal, (5) concentration, (6) wisdom, (7) making vows to benefit others, (8) protection, (9) joy, and (10) the summit experience.

Ten Nourishing Mental States

All buddhas should know that from these ten departures toward the destination, one enters into the firm patience [based on cognition of the nonarising] of dharmas, within which there are ten entries and fruitions of nourishing mental states. These are the mental states of (1) kindness, (2) pity, (3) joy, (4) detachment (5) generosity (giving), (6) good speech, (7) beneficence, (8) empathy, (9) concentration, and (10) wisdom.

Ten Adamantine Mental States

All buddhas should know that following upon these ten nourishing mental states, one enters into the entries and fruitions of the adamantine mental stages within firmly cultivated patience, the mental states of (1) faith, (2) mindfulness, (3) dedication of merit, (4) penetration, (5) directness,

(6) nonretrogression, (7) the Great Vehicle, (8) marklessness, (9) wisdom, and (10) indestructibility.

Ten Grounds

All buddhas should know that following upon these ten adamantine mental states, one enters into the entrances and fruitions of the ten grounds, which are within the firm holy patience. These are (1) the ground of equality of essential nature, (2) the ground of excellent wisdom of the essential nature, (3) the ground of the luminosity of the essential nature, (4) the ground of the knowability (*jñeya*) of the essential nature, (5) the ground of the illumination from wisdom of the essential nature, (6) the ground of the lotus radiance of the essential nature, (7) the ground of the consummation of the essential nature, (8) the ground of the Buddha's roar of the essential nature, (9) the ground of   998a
the adornment of the essential nature, and (10) the ground of entering the buddha realm of the essential nature.

As for this "Chapter on the Forty Dharmas," in a former life, when I was a bodhisattva, I practiced and entered into the source of buddha fruitions. In the same way, all sentient beings enter into the departures toward the destination, nourishing mental states, adamantine mental states, and the ten grounds, ascending to perfection. Without conditioning, without marks, there is great consummation and continuous abiding. The ten powers,[5] the eighteen distinctive practices,[6] the Dharma body, and the wisdom body are perfectly completed.

At this time, in the lotus platform store world, with Rocana Buddha sitting upon his evanescent great radiant throne, were the thousand buddhas on the flower petals, the ten trillion buddhas, the buddhas of all realms. Sitting in their midst was a bodhisattva named Flower Radiance King Great Wisdom Illumination. He rose from his seat and addressed Vairocana Buddha:

World-honored One, you have previously briefly introduced the names and characteristics of the ten stages of departure toward the destination, the ten stages of nurturance, the ten adamantine mental states, and the ten grounds. But we have not yet been able to fully understand the content of each. I entreat you to explain this. I wish only that you will explain this.

The teaching of the omniscience of the perfectly exquisite adamantine jewel store has already been explained in the "Chapter on the Tathāgata's Hundred Contemplations."

The Ten Departures toward the Destination

At this time, Vairocana Buddha said, "Thousand buddhas, please listen well. You have just asked about the meaning of this."

1. The Mental State of Detachment

Within [the ten] departures toward the destination, my disciples should practice nonattachment from all things: states, cities, homes, gold and silver, jewelry, sons and daughters, and their own selves—all conditioned things are to be abandoned, such that there is neither conditioning nor appearances. The views of self and person are only provisional combinations, subjectively constructing the view of self. The twelve links of dependent arising (*pratītyasamutpāda*) neither combine nor disperse. "No receiver" [of a donation] means that the twelve sense fields (*āyatanas*), the eighteen elements (*dhātus*), the five aggregates (*skandhas*)—all marks of conglomeration—lack the marks of self and its objects. All provisionally formed dharmas, whether internal or external, are neither relinquished nor received. At this time, for the bodhisattvas the observation of names as being nothing more than provisional combinations becomes self-evident, and therefore their detached minds enter into the *samādhi* of emptiness.

2. The Mental State of Morality

My disciples, in the mental state of morality there are [neither precepts nor] non-precepts, and [there is] no recipient of the precepts.[7] In the ten wholesome precepts there is no teacher who expounds the Dharma. From the crimes of deception[8] and stealing up to wrong views, there is no one to accumulate and receive them. Kindness, virtue, purity, straightforwardness, correctness, truth, correct views, detachment, bliss, and so forth, which are the essential nature of the ten precepts, serve to restrain one from falling into the eight inverted views.[9] Free from all natures, the single way is purified.

3. The Mental State of Patience

My disciples, patience is the essence of the wisdom of the marks of existence and nonexistence. This includes the patience of knowing the emptiness of all emptiness and the patience exercised in all situations. [The patience of all emptiness being empty] is called patience based on the [awareness of] the nonarising of activity. The patience in all situations is called patience of the knowledge that all is suffering. Each of these numberless acts is called patience. With no receiving and no striking, without violent or angry thoughts, all is simply thus; there are no separate existences, just the single mark of the truth, the mark of the nonexistence of nonexistence, the mark of existence and nonexistence, the mark of no non-mind, and the mark of objects and no objects. Whether one is standing, staying, going, or stopping (i.e., the four modes of deportment), in binding and liberation from self and person all dharmas are thus, and the marks of patience are unknowable.

998b

4. The Mental State of Zeal

My disciples, if at all times in the four modes of deportment you quell the empty and the nominal and realize the Dharma-nature, and ascend the mountain of the unproduced, you see all existents and nonexistents as seemingly existent and seemingly nonexistent. [You enter through] the universal points of orientation for contemplation, such as the earth [and the primary colors of] blue, yellow, red, and white, up to the wisdom of the Three Treasures (Buddha, Dharma, and Sangha). From all paths of effort based on faith, and from the emptiness of nonarising, nonproduction, and no wisdom, you stir yourself from emptiness and enter the Dharma of the conventional truth. Indeed, there are not two aspects [of conventional and ultimate], so the continuance of the empty mind achieves penetration and you advance to the partial attainment of wholesome roots.

5. The Mental State of Concentration

My disciples, you should be quiescent, markless, in the markless *samā-dhi* of immeasurable activity and immeasurable mind. Among worldly beings and sages there are none who do not enter [this] *samādhi*. This is because it is concomitant with their essential nature and all [practice] using the power of concentration. Self, person, doer, experiencer, all bonds, seeing essences—these are the causes and conditions of obstruction. Scattered as if by the wind, the mind is agitated and unsettled; yet when extinguished by the emptying of emptiness the eight inverted views have no place to which to link. With the meditations of calmness (*śamatha*) and insight on the nominal (*vipaśyanā*), all temporary agglomerations are extinguished from moment to moment. Experiencing their culpability for the effects engendered in the three realms, all disciples rely on the concentration of cessation and produce all kinds of wholesomeness.

6. The Mental State of Insight

My disciples, the wisdom of emptiness does not lack objects. The essence of knowing is called mind, which discriminates all dharmas. Provisionally designated as the subject, it passes through the same course. Reaping fruits and cultivating causes, one enters the holy and abandons the mundane. Destroying sins and giving rise to virtue, becoming liberated from bonds—all are the functions of this essence. All views of eternality, joy, self, purity, and afflictions occur because the essence of wisdom is not clear. With wisdom leading the way, one cultivates the inexplicable observing wisdom and enters into the single truth of the Middle Way. This ignorance obstructs wisdom. Unmarked, it does not come [from a specific place], it is not conditioned and is not sinful; it is not the eight inversions and is without arising and ceasing. The light of wisdom burns brightly in order to shed light on the vacuity of indulgence. Skillful means, transformation, and supernormal powers are regarded as the functions of wisdom by means of the essence of cognition.

7. The Mental State of Making Vows

My disciples, you should vow, and vow with great yearning, with total yearning. In order to have results you cultivate causes; therefore, the thoughts of the vow are linked; the thoughts of the vow are linked continuously, and in one hundred *kalpa*s one will attain buddhahood and one's sins will be extirpated. With wholehearted aspiration nonarising and emptiness are united. Vowing to contemplate, you contemplate, entering concentration and illumination. Because of this yearning mind, one is released from countless bonds of views. Because of this yearning mind, innumerable marvelous practices are brought to completion. The innumerable merits of *bodhi* take yearning as their root. One first arouses a yearning mind, and in the middle one cultivates the way. As your practices complete your vow you will directly attain buddhahood. In contemplating the Middle Way of the one truth, there is no illumination, no delimitation, and no extinction. Giving rise to various views   998c
is not liberating wisdom. This is the essence of the vow, the origin of all practices.

8. The Mental State of Guarding

My disciples, you should guard the Three Treasures, guard the merit of all practices, and prevent the eight inversions and the mistaken views of non-Buddhists from disturbing true faith. When you extinguish the bonds of self, the bonds of views do not come into being. Penetratingly illuminating the two truths, one observes the mind directly. By guarding the roots and through markless guarding, one guards emptiness, wishlessness, and signlessness. Using wisdom-based thoughts in a linked chain, the linked wisdom-based thoughts lead one into the state of nonproduction; the path of emptiness and the path of cognition are each brightly illuminated. Guarding contemplation and entering into emptiness, you nominally distinguish things, and that which is produced by illusion after illusion is as if nonexistent, as if nonexistent. The aggregation and dispersal of dharmic essences cannot be guarded, and so it is with the observation of dharmas.

9. The Mental State of Joy

My disciples, you should always take joy in the happiness of others. Extending to all things, you quiescently illuminate through the nominal and the empty, yet you do not enter into the conditioned and you experience no lack of quiescence. Greatly joyous without being attached to anything, you experience sensation and are transformed; you possess dharmas and see. The profound and the nominal are equal in the Dharma-nature. With singular focus you observe the mind and its functions, and you hear much about the merits of all buddha practices. Markless joyful wisdom is produced from each thought, yet it quiescently illuminates. The joyous mind connects to all dharmas.

10. The Summit Mental State

My disciples, the supreme wisdom of this person, which utterly extinguishes self and transmigration, views, doubts regarding entities, and all forms of ill-will and so forth, is summit-like. Continual contemplation is summit-like. Within the realm of cognitive experience, cause and effect being the same one path is the most excellent summit-like [mental state]. It is like the top of one's head. Views that are not nonreifying,[10] the sixty-two views, the arising and ceasing of the five aggregates; the soul, the subject, are in continual motion, contracting and expanding, without sensation and without karmic formation, without arresting and binding. At this time, one enters into the direct path of emptiness. Sentient beings in each thought see neither conditions nor nonconditions. Abiding in the summit *samādhi* of perfect cessation of thought, they begin to practice and aim for the Way. When views of essence, self, and permanence, as well as the eight inversions, appear, by connecting to the approach of nonduality one does not experience the eight difficult circumstances,[11] and finally does not experience the effects of illusion. There is only one sentient being who, whether going, coming, sitting, or standing, practices and extirpates sins, removes the ten evils, and produces the ten kinds of wholesomeness. Entering the Way as a correct person, with correct cognition, doing correct behavior, the bodhisattvas penetratingly observe that which is before them and do not undergo rebirth in the six destinies as a karmic fruit. They will definitely not fall away from the Buddha's lineage and will enter the Buddha's family in every rebirth, never departing from correct faith. This is explained in detail in the "Chapter on the Ten Celestial Illuminations" above.

The Ten Nourishing Mental States

1. The Mental State of Kindness

Vairocana Buddha said:

> Thousand buddhas, listen well! You previously inquired about the ten nurturing mental states. My disciples, always maintain an attitude of kindness. Having already produced the causes of joy in the state of the insight into selflessness, you enter dharmas by contemplation associated with joy. Such major dharmas as sensation, perception, karmic forma- 999a tion, consciousness, and form have no arising, no abiding, and no ces- sation—they are illusory, like phantasms. Since reality is not two, all practices complete the wheel of the Dharma; you transform all [sentient beings] such that they are able to give rise to correct faith and avoid evil teachings. You are also able to cause all sentient beings to attain the fruition of kindness and joy, which is neither substantial nor the result of wholesome or unwholesome activities. [This is] the *samādhi* that understands the emptiness of essences.

2. The Mental State of Pity

> My disciples, take pity as empty—empty and without marks. With pity as condition, practice the Way, automatically extinguishing all suffering. Amid the innumerable sufferings of sentient beings you produce wis- dom, not killing based on the [compassion of] the awareness of the suffering of sentient beings, not killing based on the [compassion of] the awareness of the true nature of phenomena, and not killing based on the [compassion of] nonattachment to self. If one always abstains from killing, stealing, and engaging in lust, all sentient being[s] will be unafflicted. Giving rise to the determination for enlightenment, in emptiness one sees the true characteristics of all dharmas. Amid the

13

practices at the [stage of] seed-nature one gives rise to the mental state of awareness of the Way. Amid the six intimacies,[12] the six negative intimacies, and the three grades of evil, together with superior bliss and wisdom, within the virulence of the evil conditions, there are the nine grades of attaining bliss. When the emptiness of the effects becomes clear one's own self is equal to all other sentient beings, and in one instant of bliss one gives rise to great pity.

3. The Mental State of Joy

My disciples, when you are enjoying the state of the nonproduction of thoughts, the awareness of the path of the essence of the aspects of basic proclivity [for buddhahood] is the joyous mind of emptied emptiness. Unattached to "I" and "mine," one emerges and disappears in the three divisions of time (past, present, and future) without accumulating causes and effects, and all existent things enter emptiness. The practice of contemplation is complete and one gives joy equally to all sentient beings. Giving rise to emptiness and entering the Way, one abandons unwholesome comrades and seeks out wholesome ones. Showing my favorite Way, I cause all sentient beings to enter the family of the buddha-dharma. Within the Dharma one always gives rise to joy, and within this Dharma stage, once again sentient beings enter into correct faith and abandon mistaken views. They go against the course of suffering in the six destinies, and therefore they are joyful.

4. The Mental State of Nonattachment

My disciples, you should always give rise to the mental state of nonattachment. Noncreation, marklessness, and the emptiness of dharmas are like empty space. The pairs of good and evil, having views and not having views, sinfulness and blessedness, are all equalized in a singular illumination. The negation of the personality and the negation of "I" and "mine," coupled with the unobtainability of the self-natures of self and other, result in great detachment, which extends to one's own body, flesh, hands and feet, male and female, states and cities. Like phantoms, flowing rivers, and burning lamps, one lets go of [all such objects of attachment]. Without giving rise to thought, you constantly cultivate nonattachment.

5. The Mental State of Giving

My disciples, in the mental state of giving you are able to provide
things to all sentient beings. Through giving in acts of body, speech,
and mind, giving possessions, and giving the Dharma, you guide all
sentient beings. Within one's family and outside of it, [categories of]
states and cities, male and female, farmland and domiciles—all are
marked by thusness, up to non-awareness of the object that is given,
its recipient, or its donor. There is no gathering and scattering either
internally or externally, and no thought that you are teaching others.
Through penetrating the principle and penetratingly giving, all marks
are readily apparent.

6. The Mental State of Caring Speech

My disciples, you should enter into the *samādhi* of essential caring   999b
speech—the meaning of the Dharma speech of the cardinal truth. All
true speech without exception accords with one spoken word, which
soothes the minds of all sentient beings so that they are free from both
anger and strife. The cognition of the emptiness of all dharmas, without
conditions, constantly gives rise to the mental state of gentle caring.
Your actions accord with the Buddha's intention and you also accord
with all other beings. Using the speech of the holy Dharma, you teach
all sentient beings, continually applying the mind of thusness, giving
rise to wholesome roots.

7. The Mental State of Beneficence

My disciples, you should give rise to beneficent states of mind, using
the essence of true cognition to broadly practice the path of wisdom,
gathering all brightly shining Dharma teachings, gathering the seven
[holy] assets[13] for the practice of contemplation. Since those immediately
before you have received benefit, you should also receive [this benefit]
of body and life and enter the beneficent *samādhi,* displaying all acts
of body, speech, and mind, thereby moving the great world into activity.
Through all your activities and functions, others who enter in the
Dharma seed, the emptiness seed, and the path seed will obtain benefit

and the effects of bliss. Taking form in the six destinies, undergoing immeasurable suffering—don't take this as painful; instead, see it simply as an opportunity to help others.

8. The Mental State of Sameness

My disciples, take the wisdom of the essence of the Way to be the same as the emptiness of the nonarising of dharmas. Take the wisdom of no-self to be the same as production without duality. Emptiness is the same as the original object; dharmas are marked by thusness, always arising, always abiding, always disappearing. Conventional dharmas continue in innumerable evolutions, yet they are able to manifest the activities of countless shaped bodies, form, and mind that enter into the six destinies, in all shared affairs. Emptiness is the same as nonarising, the self is the same as nothingness; yet dividing your body and scattering your form, you enter into the *samādhi* of the sameness of dharmas.

9. The Mental State of Concentration

My disciples, you should furthermore accord with the mental state of concentration. Through contemplative wisdom you witness emptiness; in each thought you calm conditions. The dharmas of "I" and "mine" [operate within] the sphere of consciousness and the sphere of form, yet remain unchanged. Through both resistance and acquiescence to the flow of samsara you continually enter the hundred *samādhi*s and the ten limbs of meditation. Using one moment of wisdom to construct this view, all selves and individuals, whether internal or external, and all the seeds of sentient beings neither combine nor disperse; they gather, take form, and arise but they are unobtainable.

10. The Mental State of Insight

My disciples, you should create the mental state of insight and observe that all fetters such as false views, active afflictions, latent afflictions, and so forth lack definitive essence. Because patient endurance [based on the realization of the birthlessness of phenomena] is the same as emptiness, they are neither the dharmas of the aggregates, elements, sense fields, or sentient beings, nor are they a unitary self; they are not cause and effect or the three times. The nature of insight produces crystal-clear illumination and a single light shines everywhere; one sees voidness, without sensation. These skillful means of insight give rise to the mental state of nurturance, and in this mental state one enters into the production of the path of the emptiness of emptiness, giving rise to the unarisen mind. The gateway to the knowledge of all dharmas has already been explained earlier in the chapter on the "Luminous King of the Thousand Seas."

The Ten Adamantine Mental States

1. The Mental State of Faith

Vairocana Buddha said: 999c

Thousand buddhas, listen well! You previously said that the adamantine seed has ten mental states. My disciples, as for faith, all practices take faith as their point of departure; it is the root of myriad virtues; it does not give rise to the mental states of the mistaken views of non-Buddhists. [In the state of faith] all views are called attachments, and [in the state of faith] one definitely does not undergo the production of karma that binds one to existence; thus you enter into the emptiness of unconditioned phenomena. The three marks are nonexistent; there is no nonarising—nonarising is nonexistent; abiding and abode do not exist, extinction and extinguished do not exist. Because there is [such a thing as] the emptiness of all dharmas, there is cognition based on conventional truth and ultimate truth; total extinction is different from emptiness; form is empty; each of the subtle aspects of mind (i.e., the other four aggregates) are empty; since the subtle aspects of mind imply the emptiness of mind, in each instance of faith they are extinguished; bereft of essence they merge together, and they are also without basis. Nonetheless, while the subject is called "self" and "person," the nominal selves of the three realms do not appropriate the marks of combination; hence, it is called "markless faith."

17

2. The Mental State of Mindfulness

My disciples, pay attention to the six kinds of mindfulness, from constant awareness up to constant bestowing, and the ultimate truth of emptiness, which has neither attachment nor liberation. The marks of arising, abiding, and extinction do not start, do not arrive, nor do they go or come. Yet [if] all those who undergo the effects of karma turn away from the habit of reification and enter the cognition of the Dharma realm, then wisdom multiplies, and as it multiplies it disappears. Each blaze is impermanent; each illumination, nothing; each production, unarisen. Change is the path of emptiness, altering the former and turning into the latter, changing, changing, turning, transforming; transforming, transforming, turning, turning; changing simultaneously in the same abode. All blazes have a single mark, arising and cessation are simultaneous. Already changed, not yet changed; changing, changing, transforming; yet incurring one reception [of karma] is also like this.

3. The Profound Mental State

My disciples, the profound mental state refers to the cardinal principle of emptiness. In the accurate cognition of the emptiness of dharmas you illuminate true existence. The continuation of the course of karma and the Middle Way of cause and effect is called real truth. The nominal designation of dharmas as subjective self and person is called conventional truth. Within these two truths of existence, one enters ever more deeply into emptiness, yet without going or coming. One illusorily experiences karmic effects, yet nothing is undergone. Therefore one experiences extremely profound mental liberation.

4. The Mental State of Penetrating Illumination

My disciples, those who penetratingly illuminate [the truth] patiently accord with all real natures. Each nature is without binding, without liberation, and without obstruction. The Dharma penetrates, the meaning penetrates, the words penetrate, and the teaching penetrates. The causes and effects of the three times and the capacities and practices of sentient beings are simply thus: they are neither united nor dispersed; they have no true function, no provisional function, no nominal function—every kind of function is totally empty. Emptied of emptiness, one penetratingly illuminates emptiness, and this is called "penetrating the emptiness of all dharmas." Since each is empty and simply thus, their marks are unobtainable.

5. The Direct Mental State

My disciples, "direct" means direct illumination. The soul that is gathered from conditions enters into the cognition of nonarising. The ignorant souls are each empty of emptiness; the mind of the principle of emptiness within emptiness resides in existence and resides in nonexistence, yet it does not damage the seeds of the Way. The uncontaminated Middle Way has just one contemplation, yet it teaches and transforms all sentient   1000a beings in the ten directions, transmitting to them all the full knowledge of the direct, true nature of emptiness. Directly practicing [the contemplation of] emptiness, those [who abide] in the three realms are conjoined [to cyclic existence] but are not subject to it.

6. The Mental State of Nonretrogression

My disciples, in the mental state of nonretrogression you do not enter into any worldly stages; you do not give rise to and nurture new views; neither do you also not habituate the causes of the semblances of self and personhood. Entering into the activities of the three realms, you cultivate the stage of emptiness without falling back, and are liberated within the supreme Middle Way. Since your practices are unified [with the supreme Middle Way], you do not retrogress in your practice. Since the original essence of all things is nondual, you do not retrogress in your mindfulness. The cognition produced from the contemplation of production from emptiness continues just as it is, and the intensified mind enters into nonduality. In the mind produced from emptiness, with one path and one purity, you never retrogress from the one path and the one illumination.

7. The Mental State of the Great Vehicle

My disciples, holding exclusively to the mind of the Great Vehicle means that because of the double understanding of the single emptiness,[14]

19

all mental states of practice are called the One Vehicle. Based in the wisdom of the one emptiness, the wisdom vehicle and the practice vehicle carry this wisdom with every thought and adaptively respond to it. They carry and adaptively respond to all sentient beings, ferrying them across the river of the three realms, across the river of bondage, across the river of arising and ceasing. The travelers are transported by the vehicle, and the wisdom mind that functions to bear and accept enters into the buddha sea. Therefore, all sentient beings who have not yet attained acceptance of the wisdom of emptiness are not called [practitioners of] the Great Vehicle; they are merely said to be in the sea of suffering, over which the vehicle is able to cross.

8. The Markless Mental State

My disciples, the markless mental state is that in which you are liberated through forgetting the marks and illuminating the nonduality of the perfection of wisdom. All bonds, karma, and the dharmas of the three times are simply thus in the one truth—yet one practices within the emptiness of nonarising. When you know for yourself the attainment of buddhahood, [you can then say that] all buddhas are the same as oneself; all worthies and sages are engaged in the same discipline as oneself. All are the same in the emptiness of nonarising, so it is called the markless mental state.

9. The Mental State of Wisdom

My disciples, "wisdom of thusness" means that in innumerable Dharma realms there is no arising, no undergoing of birth. You continuously produce afflictions but are not bound by them. All the teachings, all the paths followed by the worthies, all the dharmas contemplated by the holy ones—all of these are also just like this. All of the Buddha's skillful teaching methods are gathered in one's own mind. All the theories of non-Buddhists, the functions of mistaken meditation, illusory and mistaken explanations—the Buddha calls all these "discriminations." Entering into the bases of the two truths, they are neither one nor two and there are no aggregates, elements of cognitive activity, or perceptual fields. This wisdom radiates brightly and its bright radiance enters into all dharmas.

10. The Indestructible Mental State

My disciples, the stage of the indestructible mind is the entry into the wisdom of the grounds of the holy ones and the approach to the stage of liberation. However, on attaining the correct entry to the Way you illuminate the *bodhi*-mind (*bodhicitta*) and the patient forbearance that accords with emptiness, and cannot be damaged by the eight *māra*s. When the sages lay their hands upon your head, and you have received the buddhas' empowerment, you enter the peak *samādhi;* your body emits beams of light that illuminate the buddha lands in the ten direc- 1000b tions. Entering into the Buddha's deportment and spirit, you come and go [in and out of this world] freely, quaking a billion worlds. It is neither different nor distinguished from the mind at the ground of equality, but this is not yet the path of the wisdom of the Middle Way. Based on the power of *samādhi,* illuminating within, you see the Buddha's innu-merable lands, which manifest as sermons. At that time, you attain the peak *samādhi* and ascend to the ground of empty equality—the practice of total retention, the completion of the holy practices. In each thought you contemplate emptiness, and since there is illumination of markless-ness in the Middle Way of the wisdom of the two kinds of emptiness, all marks are extinguished. You gain access to the adamantine *samādhi* and enter the gate of all practices, which is entering into the stage of equality in emptiness. This is all explained in detail in the *Buddha Flower Sutra.*

The Ten Grounds

1. The Ground of the Equality of the Essence
Vairocana Buddha said:

Thousand buddhas, listen well! You previously asked, "What is the meaning of 'ground'?" My disciples, when bodhisattvas enter into the ground of the essence of the wisdom of equality, they teach the true Dharma. All practices reach fruition in the flower illumination that completely fills the four heavens; it is the teaching that relies on the vehicle, the teaching that relies on the nondelimited principle. The ten supernatural powers, the ten epithets, the eighteen distinctive characteristics, abiding in the Buddha's Pure Land, innumerable great vows, fearless rhetorical skill, all the sciences, all practices—I attain and enter all of these, having been born in the family of the Buddha and established on the ground of buddha-nature. In the end, neither experiencing any obstacles nor the causes and effects of ordinary people, I am filled with great bliss. From one buddha land I enter innumerable buddha lands; from one *kalpa* I enter innumerable *kalpas*; the inexplicable teachings become explicable. In reflection I see all dharmas and in resisting and complying I see all dharmas; while always entering the two truths I remain in the ultimate truth.

Through a single awareness I know the sequence of the ten grounds; in every affair I act as a sentient being, yet my mind remains in the Middle Way in each thought. Through a single awareness I know the distinctive qualities of all buddha lands, as well as the teaching expounded by these buddhas, yet my body and mind remain unchanged. Through a single awareness I know the twelve limbs of dependent arising and the seed natures of the ten unwholesome actions, yet I always maintain wholesome activity. Through a single awareness I see the aspects of both existence and nonexistence; through a single awareness I know the entry into the ten limbs of meditation and the practice of the thirty-seven factors of enlightenment, yet I manifest form bodies throughout the six destinies. Through a single awareness I know every single form in the ten directions, each fully arising separately; entering into the retribution of the reception of form, yet never tethered in any single thought. My radiance illuminates everything; hence, there is no birth. Firm belief[15] and the wisdom of emptiness are always present before me; from the first ground and the second ground up to the realm of the Buddha, all the Dharma approaches in between are practiced concurrently. In summary, the practices and vows of the ocean-store of merits of the ground of equality are like the tip of a hair on a bubble in the ocean.

2. The Ground of the Skillful Wisdom of the Essence

My disciples, bodhisattvas at the ground of the skillful wisdom of the essence purify and fully illuminate all wholesome roots. Kindness, pity, joy, nonattachment [to one's own possessions], and wisdom are the roots of all merit.

Starting from the first contemplation, one enters into the cognition of the path of skillful means of the wisdom of great emptiness and sees that there are no sentient beings not subject to the truth of suffering. All possess a conscious mind and feel all of the suffering and distress of the swords and staves of the three evil destinies. Within these conditions they produce consciousness; this is called the truth of suffering. As for the characteristics of the three kinds of suffering, the first is the initial bodily awareness [arising] from [experiencing] the swords and staves and the aggregate of bodily form; within these two conditions awareness arises, serving as the condition for suffering due to the compounded nature of existence. Next, since that which is conditioned by awareness in conscious thought and awareness of the conditioned body appropriates the swords and staves as well as bodily sores and ulcers and so forth, you are aware of the conditions of compounded suffering.[16] Since suffering is doubled, it is called compounded suffering. Next, being aware of sensation and karmic flux these two mental conditions support each other, and within the deterioration and sores experienced in the aggregate of bodily form one gives rise to an awareness of suffering; therefore, this is called the condition of suffering of deterioration. Based on these three awarenesses, one produces three mental states in this sequence, So it is called "suffering on top of compounded suffering."

Because all sentient beings that possess a mind who see these three kinds of suffering give rise to the causes and conditions for immeasurable suffering and distress, I enter into the *samādhi* of the path of teaching and conversion. I manifest form bodies throughout the six destinies and elucidate the approaches to the Dharma with the ten kinds of rhetorical skill. This means that in "awareness of suffering" and "conditions for suffering," the conditions of [the physical pain caused by] swords and staves are included. In awareness of suffering in the

1000c

conditioned bodily sores and decay impinge internally and externally; sometimes they are included and sometimes not. Within the inclusion of these two conditions, consciousness is produced and consciousness creates; consciousness senses, impinging on consciousness—this is called the consciousness of suffering. Since it karmically forms two conditions, each thought conditions form; the mind impinges; impingement brings distress. At the moment one feels this pain and distress it is called "compounded suffering." Mind, conditions, and consciousness first abide in faculties being aware of conditions; this is called "awareness of suffering." The mind creates and the mind feels, it impinges on consciousness and awareness of it [further] impinges; when one has not yet felt this pain and distress (i.e., compounded suffering) it is called "suffering induced by karmic flux."

Impingement produces awareness, just as hewing a stone produces sparks. In the moment-to-moment arising and cessation in body and mind, the body disintegrates, changes, and transforms, while consciousness is subjected to the disintegration of conditions. Conditions gather and scatter, and after mental pain and mental anxiety are felt and noted, they subsequently condition so as to pollute and attach, never being relinquished for even a single thought-moment. This is the suffering of decay. The three realms are nothing but the truth of suffering. If we further analyze ignorance, one accumulates innumerable thoughts, creating all kinds of karma that continue without interruption, habituating causes and gathering causes. This is called the truth of arising. Liberation through right view, the path of discernment of both kinds of emptiness in each thought, is called the truth of the Way by means of the path of discernment. All karmic retribution and all causal purity that exist are illuminated at once in their essential natures; this is the one truth of extinction by subtle discernment. Being fully endowed with the qualities of wisdom is called the "root." The essence of all wisdom, giving rise to emptiness, enters contemplation. This is the first wholesome root.

In the second, one contemplates the relinquishment of all kinds of craving and attachment, practicing all forms of relinquishment based on [awareness of] the equality of emptiness. Without conditions one sees all dharmas to have the single aspect of the state of emptiness:

I see all lands in the ten directions to be the former lands that I enjoyed in previous lives. The waters of the four great seas are all my former waters; all age-ending conflagrations are the conflagrations I formerly applied in my previous lives. All whirlwinds are the ethers I formerly employed. I now enter into this world with my Dharma body complete, relinquishing my former body. In the end I will not take on my former impure limited body composed of the four elements.

1001a

This is the consummation of the faculty of relinquishment.

The third is the contemplation of all sentient beings that are transformed, in conjunction with the joy of human and celestial existence, the joy of the ten grounds, the joy of freedom of fear of the ten evil forms of behavior, and the joy of attainment of the marvelous flower *samādhi,* up to the joy of buddhahood. This kind of contemplation is the consummation of the faculty of compassion. At this time bodhisattvas abiding in this ground have neither delusion, nor craving, nor ill-will, and they enter into the cognition of the single truth of equality—the root of all practices. Buddhas traverse throughout all worlds, manifesting innumerable Dharma bodies.

This is as explained in the "Chapter on the Heavenly Flower of All Sentient Beings."

3. The Ground of the Luminosity of the Essence

My disciples, bodhisattvas at the ground of the luminosity of the essence use *samādhi* and complete understanding to know all the Buddha's teachings of the three times, the words, meanings, and phrases of the twelve divisions of the canon: repeating verses, predictions, straight narrative, pure verse, uninvited sermons, rules and disciplines, parables, buddha realms, ancient matters, corrective, never before seen, and conversations. This is the essence of the Dharma, with words specifying all meanings.

All conditioned dharmas are explained within these words, meanings, and phrases. They are born bit by bit, starting with the entry of consciousness into the womb and the four elements that enliven the material

25

and mental [factors]. Names and the six [sense] bases within the faculties produce raw awareness, which, having not yet discriminated suffering and pleasure, is called "contact consciousness." Furthermore, the consciousness of suffering, pleasure, and consciousness is called the "three sensations"; one is continually aware of and endlessly attached to sensation. Through grasping desire, self, views, and precepts, good and evil come into existence. The advent of consciousness is called birth; the end of consciousness is called death. These ten items are the contemplation of the causes, conditions, and effects of present suffering.

[In this] mode of appearance [of contemplation of dependent arising], by means of the Middle Way I have been free for a long time and have no sense of own-nature. Entering into luminous supernatural powers, total retention, and eloquence, I contemplate emptiness in all thoughts, and in the present *kalpa* in the buddha lands of the ten directions I teach others, enlightening others for a hundred *kalpa*s, a thousand *kalpa*s. In these lands I nourished supernatural abilities, paying obeisance before the Buddha and requesting to hear words of Dharma. I furthermore appear in bodies throughout the six destinies and in a single voice explain countless aspects of the Dharma. Yet each sentient being, according to his or her particular spiritual proclivities, hears the Dharma he or she wants to hear. Suffering, emptiness, impermanence, and no-self are the sounds of the one truth [of suffering]. Their lands are not the same, their bodies and minds are transformed in distinctive ways.

What is explained here in this ground of illumination of the marvelous flower is nothing more than a summary that is like [a single strand] of hair. Its full elaboration is like that explained in the "Dharma Chapter" and in the "Liberation Contemplation Dharma Gate Thousand *Samādhi* Chapter."

4. The Ground of the Knowability of the Essence

My disciples, bodhisattvas in the stage of essence accord with the real and illuminate the conventional, without annihilating or holding to eternalism; at the same time arising, abiding, and extinguishing; each lifetime, each moment, and each existence are differentiated. Since they appear differently, the middle way of causes and conditions is neither one nor two, neither good nor bad. Since they are neither worldlings nor buddhas, the realms of the buddhas and the realms of worldlings are distinguished, one by one. This is called conventional truth. In this view of the way of discernment there is neither one nor two; the profound Way and the category of concentration. The mental functions of the buddhas are, at first, the awareness of concentration as cause; then faith awareness, thought awareness, still awareness, upward awareness, remembrance awareness, wisdom awareness, contemplation awareness, pliant awareness, comfortable awareness, and indifferent awareness. These various categories of the path of skillful means enter in each thought into the concentration result; these people, abiding in concentration, vividly see the emptiness of the activity of dharmas. If they give rise to mindful concentration they enter into the production of thought concentration, produce loving accordance with the Way, and following the Dharma they teach people. This is called tolerance of joy in the Dharma, tolerance of abiding, tolerance of realization, and tolerance of extinction.

1001b

Therefore the buddhas, entering the radiant flower *samādhi,* manifest innumerable buddhas who, placing their hands on the heads of the listeners, expound the Dharma with a single voice. In a hundred thousand stirrings they do not depart from concentration. They abide in concentration, enjoy the flavor of concentration, are addicted to concentration, and crave concentration. Abiding in concentration in one *kalpa* or a thousand *kalpa*s, these people see buddhas on lotus thrones expounding a hundred approaches to the Dharma. These people make offerings and listen to the Dharma, abiding in concentration for a single *kalpa.* At this time, within the buddhas' luminosity they receive the laying on of the buddhas' hands on their heads and give rise to the state of concentration, the aspect of transcendence, the aspect of advancement, and the aspect of tending toward. So they do not sink down and do not retreat; they do not fall and they do not linger. In the Dharma of the peak *samādhi* there is tolerance of superior bliss, permanent extinction without remainder. Thereupon, entering into all buddha lands they cultivate themselves in the category of innumerable merits, each practice luminously shining. Entering into the application of skillful means, they enlighten all sentient beings, enabling them to gain a vision of the constancy, bliss, self, and purity of buddha-nature. These people who are born in and abide in this land carry out the Dharma teachings of conversion, which become gradually more profound. With knowledge of the contemplation of sky-flowers they enter the Middle Way of the essence, and the "Chapter on all the Approaches to the Dharma" is fulfilled. It is just like the adamant mentioned in the previous "Chapter on the Course of the Sun and Moon," in which this point has already been explained.

5. The Ground of the Wisdom-illumination of the Essence

My disciples, for bodhisattvas at the ground of the essence of wisdom illumination, the Dharma has qualities produced from ten kinds of powers, which give rise to all meritorious activities. By one activity of the skillful means of wisdom, one knows the distinction of good and evil activities; this is the category of the power of [knowing] what is appropriate. [Knowledge of] the karma from good and evil activities is called the category of knowledge power. [Knowledge of] all the desires and aspirations of all beings in the six destinies is called the category of the power of [knowledge of] the fruits desired. [Knowledge of] the distinction of the natures of beings in the six destinies is the category of the power of [knowledge of] the natures. [Knowledge of] the distinction of faculties as being wholesome or unwholesome is the category of the power of the [knowledge of] the faculties. [Knowledge of] the wrongly determined, correctly determined, and undetermined is called the category of [knowledge of] determination. [Knowing that] in all the causes and effects [in the path] the vehicle is the cause and the vehicle is the effect, and that reaching the effect is based in the vehicle that is the cause of the path—this is the category of the power of the [knowledge of] the path. The five eyes know all dharmas and see the undergoing of all rebirths; hence the category of the power of the [knowledge of the] divine eye. Every single matter of a thousand *kalpa*s is known; this is the category of the power of [knowledge of] previous lives. [Knowledge of] the extinction of all active afflictions and the extinction of all received ignorance—this is the category of the power of [the knowledge of] liberation. The knowledge of these ten categories of powers is to know one's own cultivation of causes and fruition, as well as to know the distinction in the causes and fruitions of all sentient beings.

Yet the distinct functions of body, speech, and mind take the Pure Land as an evil land and take evil lands as paradise. They are able to turn the wholesome into the unwholesome, and the unwholesome into the wholesome. They take form as nonform and nonform as form; males are taken as female, females are taken as male. The six destinies are taken as being other than the six destinies, and that which is other than the six destinies is taken as the six destinies. And so forth, up to earth, water, fire, and wind not being earth, water, fire, and wind. At this time, this person takes the power of great skillful means and goes along with all sentient beings. Yet he sees the inconceivable, that which is unknowable to those at lower stages, the awareness of all the mundane affairs of life.

1001c

This person's great bright wisdom gradually advances; discriminating cognition illuminates again and again, immeasurably and immeasurably. Inexplicable, ineffable approaches to the Dharma are right before him.

6. The Ground of the Floral Radiance of the Essence

My disciples, bodhisattvas at the ground of the floral radiance of the essence are able, in all realms, to avail themselves of the ten kinds of supernatural cognitive powers in order to manifest various forms for all sentient beings. (1) Through knowledge of the divine eye, one knows all the lands in the three divisions of time; one knows all the infinitesimal bits of form that combine bit by bit to constitute the bodies of the sentient beings within the six destinies; every single body's infinitesimal subtle forms that materialize great form are known bit by bit. (2) Through knowledge of the divine ear, one knows the sounds and the cries of suffering and pleasure coming from the sentient beings in the six destinies in the ten directions and three divisions of time; one knows not non-sounds and not non-voices—all Dharma voices. (3) Through knowledge of the divine body, one knows all forms, forms and nonforms, neither male nor female forms; in one thought-moment, one functions in innumerable bodies in lands and eons throughout the ten directions and the three divisions of time, in great and small lands.

(4) Through the divine knowledge of the minds of others, one knows the activities within the minds of sentient beings in the three divisions of time; one knows the content of each thought of all sentient beings in the six destinies of the ten directions—all matters of pain and pleasure, good and evil. (5) Through divine knowledge of humans, one knows the past lives, the pain and pleasure, and the future rebirths of all sentient beings in all the lands in the ten directions and the three divisions of time; one knows every single life continuing for a hundred *kalpa*s. (6) Through divine knowledge of liberation, one knows the liberation of sentient beings in the ten directions and the three divisions of time; the removal of all afflictions, whether numerous or few; from the first ground up to the tenth ground all are completely extinguished, one after another.

(7) Through divine knowledge of meditative states one knows the meditative and nonmeditative states of the minds of all sentient beings in the lands of the ten directions and in the three divisions of time; one also knows the nonmeditative as well as the not-nonmeditative states, the methods of producing meditative states along with all included states of *samādhi,* the one hundred kinds of *samādhi.* (8) Through divine knowledge of enlightenment one knows the attainment of enlightenment and the nonattainment of enlightenment by all sentient beings, up to knowing the minds of every person in the six destinies, and also knowing the Dharma that is expounded in the minds of the buddhas of the ten directions. (9) Through divine knowledge of recollection, one knows the lives of sentient beings throughout a hundred *kalpa*s, a thousand *kalpa*s, and within greater and lesser *kalpa*s, whether these lives are long or short. (10) Through divine knowledge of aspirations, one knows every single aspiration and resolve of the sages of the ten grounds and the adepts of the thirty stages; whether seeking pain or pleasure, the Dharma or non-Dharma—all kinds of seeking—completely, including the ten vows and the hundred thousand great vows. This person, abiding in the grounds, with access to the ten supernormal abilities manifests countless distinct functions of action, speech, and

thought, which are called the merits of the grounds and which cannot be exhausted in ten billion *kalpas*. Yet it is precisely these upon which Śākyamuni has expounded in a concise manner in the "Chapter on Supernormal Abilities." This is the same as that which is explained in the "Chapter on the Contemplation of the Twelve Limbs of Dependent Arising."

7. The Ground of the Completion of the Essential Nature

My disciples, when bodhisattvas [arrive at] the ground of the essence of completion, they enter into this dharma of the category of the cognition of the eighteen noble ones, which is not shared with practitioners of the lower grounds. This means that in bodily activity there is no taint or error, in verbal activity there is no fault in speech, and in thought there is no loss of mindfulness. Free from the eight [difficult] circumstances one is dispassionate in all circumstances, always remaining in *samādhi*. On entering this ground there are six kinds of endowment and, furthermore, from this your cognition produces awareness of six kinds of completion. Since you are finally not subjected to the afflictive habit energies of the three realms, your wishes are fulfilled. Since all of the merits and all of the Dharma teachings that you seek are fulfilled, effort is fulfilled. Since all Dharma matters, matters of the epoch, and the affairs of sentient beings are known in one instant, in one thought, mindfulness is fulfilled. Since the characteristics of the two truths include all the dharmas of the sentient beings in the six destinies, wisdom is fulfilled. Since you know that the people in the ten stages of opening up a clear destination, as well as all buddhas, are neither bound nor habituated, liberation is fulfilled. Since you see that all sentient beings know other sentient beings as their own disciples, and since you lack contamination and are without afflicted habituation, and since with your acumen you know other persons, liberation is fulfilled.

This person enters into these six kinds of completion of supernormal cognition and directly gives rise to the cognition wherein his body accords with the mental functioning of the sentient beings in the six destinies. Since with his mouth he skillfully elucidates the "Chapter on Innumerable Dharma Gates," teaching all sentient beings, he accords with the mental function of all sentient beings. He always enters *samādhi* while the great earth quakes in the ten directions. Since empty space becomes [adorned with] flowers, he is able, using the endowment of great illumination, to cause the mental functioning of sentient beings to see the appearance of buddhas in the world in all past *kalpa*s. Here, using unattached cognition, he also reveals the minds of all sentient beings, showing them the minds and mental functions of all buddhas and sentient beings in all the lands in the ten directions of the present. Using supernormal cognition and knowledge of the path, he sees the appearance in the world of all buddhas in all future *kalpa*s. All sentient beings accept the Way and hear the Dharma from this buddha.

Abiding in this level of the eighteen noble ones, one is in *samādhi* in every mental moment, observing the atoms of the three realms to be the causes of your own body and seeing all sentient beings as your father and mother. This is because even though I am entering into this ground, I have already entered all merits, all divine illuminations, all teachings carried out by the buddhas, up to the category of all the Dharma teachings in the eighth and ninth grounds. In all buddha lands one demonstrates the Buddha's attainment of enlightenment, his turning of the wheel of the Dharma, his entry into extinction, and his transformation of [beings] in all other lands in the past, present, and future.

1002b

8. The Ground of the Buddha's Roar of the Essential Nature

My disciples, when bodhisattvas [enter] the ground of the Buddha's roar of the essential nature, they enter into the *samādhi* of the stage of the Dharma King; their accurate cognition is like that of the Buddha, since it is the Buddha's roar *samādhi*. The ten kinds of eminently clear approaches of concentration are always directly accessible; with the sound of the flower radiance one enters the mental state of *samādhi*.

The term "wisdom of emptiness" refers to the approach of the wisdom of internal emptiness, the approach of the wisdom of external emptiness, the approach of the wisdom of the emptiness of the conditioned, the approach of the wisdom of the emptiness of the unconditioned, the approach of the wisdom of emptiness in nature, the approach of the wisdom of beginningless emptiness, the approach of the wisdom

32

of emptiness as the ultimate truth, the approach of the wisdom of the emptiness of emptiness, the approach of the wisdom that the emptiness of emptiness is again empty, and the approach of the wisdom that the emptiness of emptiness is again empty of emptiness. These ten approaches to emptiness are not known in the lower grounds. The ground of space-like equality is inexplicable, inexplicable.

The cognition of the Way through supernormal power means that with one moment of cognition one is able to know and discriminate all dharmas; entering into innumerable buddha lands, one requests elucidation of the Dharma directly before each buddha. One activates the Dharma to save all sentient beings and, in applying the medicine of the Dharma to all sentient beings, one serves as a great Dharma preacher and great spiritual guide, obliterating the four *māra*s. With one's Dharma body complete, you continually manifest physically, entering into buddha realms. Those in the category of Buddha and those in the category of the ninth and tenth grounds nourish their Dharma bodies. One hundred thousand *dhāraṇī* entrances, one hundred thousand *samādhi* entrances, one hundred thousand adamantine entrances, one hundred thousand entrances through supernormal powers, one hundred thousand liberation entrances—these are the same as these one hundred thousand entrances of space-like equality. The great unimpededness is exercised in one thought, in one instant.

*Kalpa*s are explained as non-*kalpa*s, non-*kalpa*s are explained as *kalpa*s. The non-Way is explained as the Way, the Way is explained as the non-Way. What are not the six destinies of sentient beings are explained as the six destinies of sentient beings; the six destinies of sentient beings are explained as not being the six destinies of sentient beings. Non-buddhas are explained as buddhas, buddhas are explained as non-buddhas.

Yet entering and leaving the reflection within the *samādhi* of all buddha essences, there is illumination of sequence and illumination of reversal; there is illumination of the prior and illumination of the latter, illumination of causes and illumination of effects, illumination of emptiness and illumination of existence, and illumination of the cardinal truth of the Middle Way. This kind of cognition is only realized at the level of the eighth ground—it is not something that is attained at lower stages. One neither moves nor stops, neither leaves nor enters, is neither born nor extinguished. The qualities of the Dharma entrances at this ground are numberless, numberless; inexplicable, inexplicable. Now, this brief opening up of the contents of this ground is as as rare as one strand of hair among of a hundred thousand strands of hair on the head. This has already been explained in the "Chapter on Arhats."

9. The Ground of the Flower Ornamentation of the Essence

My disciples, when bodhisattvas reach the ground of flower ornamentation of the essence, they use the buddhas' deportment and the Tathāgata's royal concentration—where they have complete control over *samādhi,* entering and leaving regardless of the time.

In the trichiliocosms of the ten directions, ten billion suns and moons, ten billion continents beneath the four heavens, in one instant they attain enlightenment, turn the wheel of the Dharma [and pass through the other eight major junctures of the Buddha's career,] up to entering into nirvana. All buddha works are manifested for all sentient beings through this one instant within one mind. All of their form bodies [exhibit] the eighty minor and thirty-two major marks; they experience unimpeded enjoyment, the same as empty space, brightly shining their immeasurable great compassion, adorned by their distinguishing and fine marks. They are neither celestial nor human, nor any of the other types of beings of the six destinies; they are beyond all dharmas yet always coursing through the six destinies, manifesting innumerable bodily [activities], innumerable verbal [activities], and innumerable [activities] of thought in order to explain innumerable approaches to the Dharma.

1002c

Yet they are able to make the transition from *māra* realms into buddha realms, from buddha realms into *māra* realms. They are to make the transition from all views to enter into the buddha view, and from the buddha view to enter into all views. From buddha-nature they enter into the natures of sentient beings, and from the natures of sentient beings they enter buddha-nature. This ground is lustrously illuminated, with wisdom after wisdom shining; brightly burning, brightly burning, they are without fear and without limitation. The stage includes the ten powers, the eighteen distinctive abilities, liberation, nirvana, and the purity of the unconditioned single path. And to all sentient beings they appear as father, mother, and elder and younger siblings and expound the Dharma for them, exhausting all *kalpa*s to attain realization of the path. They furthermore materialize in all lands and cause all sentient beings to see each other as their fathers and mothers, and to cause all *māra*s and non-Buddhists to see each other as their fathers and mothers. Abiding in this ground they start off from the state of birth and death, arriving at the adamantine state. In the space of a single thought they manifests this kind of activity and are able to transition themselves to enter the innumerable realms of sentient beings. This brief recapitulation of this kind of immeasurable activity is like a drop in the ocean.

10. The Ground of Entry into the Buddha Realm of the Essential Nature

My disciples, when bodhisattvas enter the ground of the buddha realm of the essential nature, their great wisdom is emptied; it is emptied and further emptied of emptiness, and again emptied, like the nature of space. With the cognition of equality in nature and the possession of tathāgata-nature, they are fully equipped with the ten kinds of merit. Since emptiness has the same single mark, the essential nature is unconditioned and spiritual transparency embodies oneness. Since the Dharma is the same as the Dharma-nature he is called the Thus Come One (tathā-gata). One should accord with the Four Noble Truths and the two truths, exhausting the state of cyclic existence. Dharma nourishing and the Dharma body are not two: thus he is called Worthy of Offerings (arhat). Pervasively covering all phenomena within all realms, correct cognition and holy liberative cognition know the existence or not of all dharmas, as well as the religious faculties of all sentient beings; thus he is called Correctly and Peerlessly Enlightened (*samyak-saṃbuddha*). Luminous wisdom and practices are perfected at the stage of buddhahood; thus he is called Perfected in Wisdom and Practice (*vidyā-caraṇa-saṃpanna*). Well gone in the buddha-dharma of the three times, his Dharma is the same as that of past buddhas. At the time of the past buddhas' departure they did so well, did so well, and when they came, they did so well, did so well—thus the name Well Gone (*sugata*).

His actions are the most virtuous, and entering into society he teaches sentient beings, leading them to liberation from all bonds; thus he is called Liberator of the World. This person, above all dharmas, enters into the Buddha's comportment with the appearance of a buddha. The defining activity of a great person is that of liberating people from the world. Thus he is called Unsurpassed Personage (*anuttara*). He soothes all sentient beings, who are called "souls"; [thus he is called Tamer of Souls (*puruṣadamya-sārathi*)]. Amid gods and humans he teaches all

1003a   sentient beings so that they listen to the words of the Dharma; thus he is called Teacher of Humans and Gods (*śāstā devamanuṣyānām*). The mystery and the source are not two; buddha-nature and profound awakening are always constantly greatly fulfilled; all sentient beings worship and respect him; thus he is called World-honored One. Since all the people of the world listen to and memorize the teaching, this is the buddha stage. It is within this buddha stage that all sages enter their spheres of activity; thus it is called the stage of the buddha realm.

At this time, sitting on jeweled lotuses, all [those in attendance] received assurance [of their future enlightenment] and were overjoyed. As the Dharma-body Buddha stroked their heads, bodhisattvas of the same views and learning, with different mouths yet in the same voice praised He Who is Without Equal. Furthermore, all the buddhas and bodhisattvas in the ten trillion worlds gathered like clouds, requesting the turning of the ineffable wheel of the Dharma, the Dharma approach with the guidance of Ākāśagarbha. This ground was that of the category of the inexplicable marvelous Dharma approach, the marvelous *samādhi* approach of the three kinds of supranormal cognition, and the *dhāraṇī* approach, all of which are unknowable to the minds of ordinary people in the lower stages. Only the Buddha's immeasurable deeds, speech, and thought can fathom its source. As is explained in the "Chapter on the Heaven of Radiant Sound," the ten forms of fearlessness and the buddha path are the same.

Fascicle Two

The Precepts

Preface to the Bodhisattva Precepts
of the *Brahmā's Net Sutra*

All you disciples of the Buddha, join your palms in reverence and listen whole-heartedly. I would now like to articulate the preface to the great precepts of the buddhas. If the members of the assembly will quietly listen, and they know that they have sinned, they will repent. If they repent, then they will be at ease. If they do not repent, their crimes will grow more grievous. The sinless are silent, and because of their silence you should know that they are all purified.

Worthy monks, laymen, laywomen, and all the rest, listen well! In the age of the semblance Dharma after the Buddha's passing into nirvana, you should revere the *Prātimokṣa*. The *Prātimokṣa* is none other than these precepts. When you observe these precepts, it is like darkness meeting with light; it is like a poor man becoming rich; it is like someone who is ill being healed; it is like a prisoner being released from his chains; it is like a traveler who is able to return home. You should know that these rules (i.e., the *Prātimokṣa*) are the great teacher for this assembly of people, and even if the Buddha were still in the world it would be no different. Thoughts of fear are difficult to produce; wholesome thoughts are difficult to give rise to.

Therefore a sutra says, "Do not trivialize minor misdeeds as if they are not problematic. Drops of water, although tiny, will gradually fill a large basin." A single instant of sin can lead you to fall into the hell of uninterrupted suffering. Once you lose your human body you won't get another one for ten thousand *kalpa*s. Just as a galloping horse [passes by swiftly], one's physical strength will not remain—the transience of human life goes beyond the mountains and seas. Even if something remains for the duration of one day, it will be quite difficult to hold onto it tomorrow.

Members of the assembly should each energetically advance their own minds. Be careful not to be lazy, negligent, drowsy, or arbitrary. In the evening

1003b you must gather your thoughts and focus them firmly on the Three Treasures. Don't take as being a waste of time the effort to deepen your repentance for those of later generations. Members of the assembly, each of you in your own minds should carefully rely on these precepts. Discipline yourselves in the practices that accord with the Buddha's teachings.

Invocation

At this time for the members of this great assembly, Vairocana Buddha revealed in abbreviated form the mind-ground within the ineffable Dharma gates equal in number to the grains of sand in a hundred thousand Ganges Rivers, as if making them fit on the tip of a single strand of hair.

[Vairocana said:]

> This is what all buddhas of the past have taught, what the buddhas of the future will teach, and what the buddha of the present is now teaching. It is what the bodhisattvas of the three divisions of time have already learned, what they will learn, and what they are learning. I have already cultivated this mind-ground for a hundred *kalpa*s, thus receiving the name of Rocana.[17] O buddhas, transmit what I have taught and open up the path of the mind-ground for all sentient beings.

At that time, on the brightly blazing, divinely illuminated lion's throne of the world of the lotus flower platform store, Vairocana emitted effulgent light. He addressed the thousand buddhas who were seated on the lotus petals:

> Hold on to the "Chapter on the Dharma Approach" of my mind-ground and depart. Again, you will become ten trillion Śākyas, extending this teaching to sentient beings, gradually explaining this "Chapter on the Dharma Approach of the Mental Stages." You should all memorize and recite it and, with one mind, put it into practice.

The Teaching Transmitted to the Transformation-body Buddhas

At this time the thousand buddhas sitting on lotus petals and the ten trillion Śākyas got up from the blazing lion thrones in the lotus flower store world and each returned [to his original place]. Their entire bodies emitted inconceivably numerous rays of light, and in each of these there appeared innumerable

38

buddhas. At once, they took innumerable blue, yellow, red, and white lotuses and offered these to Vairocana Buddha. Having finished receiving and memorizing the above-taught "Chapter on the Dharma Access of the Mind-ground," each took his leave and departed from this lotus flower store world.

Repayment of Kindness
and a Separate Iteration
of the Teaching

On their departure they entered the essential nature space lotus-radiance *samādhi* and returned to their original worlds, beneath the *bodhi* tree in Jambudvīpa. They then emerged from the space lotus-radiance *samādhi* of the essential nature. Having emerged, they sat on the throne illuminated by the adamantine thousand rays of light in the hall of marvelous radiance, and expounded the ten world-oceans. Rising from their seats again, they went to Indra's palace to expound the ten abodes. They again rose from their seats and proceeded to Yama Heaven, where they expounded the ten practices. Rising from their seats again, they proceeded to the fourth heaven, where they expounded the ten dedications of merit. Rising from their seats again, they proceeded to Nirmāṇarati (Creation of Enjoyment) Heaven, where they expounded the ten meditations. Rising from their seats again, they proceeded to Paranirmitavaśavartin (Partaking of Pleasures Created in Other Heavens) Heaven, where they expounded the ten grounds. They further proceeded to the first meditation, where they expounded the ten indestructible [states of mind]. They further proceeded to the second meditation, where they expounded the ten forms of tolerance. They further proceeded to the third meditation, where they expounded the ten vows. They further proceeded to the royal palace of Maheśvara within the fourth meditation, where they expounded the "Chapter on the Dharma Approach of the Mind-ground" that was explained by Vairocana Buddha in our place of origin, the lotus treasury world. The remaining ten trillion Śākyas followed suit without duality or distinction, as is explained in the "*Bhadrakalpa* Chapter."

1003c

Then Śākyamuni Buddha, after first appearing in the lotus treasury world, entered the palace of the *deva* kings from the East. After expounding the *Sutra of Māra's Conversion,* he descended to be born in the state of Kapilavastu in the southern continent of Jambudvīpa. His mother was named Māyā, his father Śuddhodana, and he himself was named Siddhārtha. He left home at the age of seven;[18] he attained enlightenment at thirty and came to be called Śākyamuni Buddha. At the site of his enlightenment he sat on the adamantine splendorous royal throne, and from that time until his ascent to the palace of the Heaven of Maheśvara, he expounded his teachings in ten places, one after the other. At this time the Buddha observed the net of Indra, the king of Brahmā Heaven, and was motivated to say:

> Innumerable worlds are just like the eyelets in this net. Each and every world is different from the other and the differences are innumerable. It is the same with the Buddha's teachings. Up to now I have returned to this world eight thousand times.
>
> For the sentient beings in this *sahā* world I have sat upon the adamantine splendorous throne [and all the other ten stations], up to the palace of King Maheśvara. I have completed the succinct disclosure of the "Chapter on the Dharma Gate of the Mind-ground." Thereafter, I descended from the heavenly palace to the place below the *bodhi* tree in Jambudvīpa, and for all the sentient beings and benighted worldlings of this world I explained the single admonishment that was always recited by our original teacher, Vairocana Buddha, when he gave rise to his original intention for enlightenment within the original mind-ground.

The Exhortation

The radiant adamantine precepts are the source of all buddhas, the origin of all bodhisattvas, the seed of buddha-nature. All sentient beings without exception possess buddha-nature. All [those who have] mentation, consciousness, form, and mind—who have these feelings and these minds—are all encompassed by these buddha-nature precepts. It is precisely because of these ever-present causes [in the form of the precepts] that there is, without fail, always an abiding Dharma body. In this way, these ten *Prātimokṣa*s[19] appear in the world, and these Dharma rules are received and upheld with reverence by all sentient beings of the three times. I will now once again recite the "Chapter on the Ten Inexhaustible Precepts Treasury" for this great assembly. These are the precepts for all sentient beings, whose original self-nature is pure.

The Bodhisattva Precepts

The Transmission and Remembrance of the Founding Teacher

Now I, Vairocana, sitting on the lotus flower platform,

On the thousand petals that surround me a thousand Śākyamunis   1004a
again appear.

Each flower has ten billion lands, and in each land a Śākyamuni.

Each sits under a *bodhi* tree, and simultaneously they all attain full
enlightenment.

These hundreds of thousands of millions of buddhas are all the
original body of Vairocana.

To each of these hundreds of thousands of millions of Śākyamunis
is attached a vast number of followers,

Who all together come to my place and listen to me recite the
Buddha's precepts.

The nectar gate is then opened, and at this time hundreds of thousands
of millions [of Śākyamunis]

Return to their original site of enlightenment, each sitting under a
bodhi tree.

Reciting the precepts of my original teacher—the ten grave and the
forty-eight [minor.]

The precepts radiate like the sun and moon; they are like jewels in a
necklace.

Vast numbers of bodhisattvas achieve perfect enlightenment based
on them.

What Vairocana recites, I also recite.

You newly initiated bodhisattvas should receive and observe the
moral discipline with great reverence.

Once you have received and observed this moral discipline, you
should impart it to all sentient beings.

Listen well, as I precisely recite the store of the moral discipline
within the Buddha's teachings—the *Prātimokṣa*.

All of you in the great assembly should believe truly in your hearts

That you will, in the future, become buddhas; I have already
become a buddha.

Once you have generated this kind of faith, then the category of
moral discipline is already complete.

All those possessed of mind should embrace the Buddha's precepts;

Sentient beings who receive the Buddha's precepts directly enter
into the buddha stages,

The stage that is identical to great enlightenment is complete—
these are truly my disciples.

All those in the great assembly should be reverent and listen with
all their hearts to my recitation.

Preface to the Formation
of the Precepts

Interlocutor's Preface

At this time Śākyamuni Buddha first sat beneath the *bodhi* tree and
achieved peerless enlightenment. [After this] his first act was to establish the
Prātimokṣa, [encouraging his followers] to piously obey their fathers and
mothers, honored monks, and the Three Treasures. Pious obedience is the
principle of the ultimate path. "Piety" is synonymous with "moral discipline,"
and also means "restraint." The Buddha then emitted immeasurable rays of
light from his mouth, and at that time a great crowd of millions of billions
of bodhisattvas, beings from the eighteen Brahmā heavens, beings from the
six heavens of the desire realm, and the kings of the sixteen major states, all
clasped their hands together in utmost reverence and listened to the Buddha
recite the Great Vehicle precepts of all buddhas.

The Preface of the World-honored One

The Preface of the Preceptor

The Buddha addressed the bodhisattvas:

I will henceforth recite the Dharma precepts of the Buddha once every
half-month. All of you bodhisattvas who have given rise to the aspiration
[for enlightenment] should also recite them, as well as the bodhisattvas
in the ten stages of departure for the destination, the ten stages of nurturance, the ten adamantine stages, and the ten grounds—all of these
bodhisattvas should also recite them. Therefore, the light of the precepts

1004b

shines forth from my mouth, so that those with affinity have no lack of cause.

The Dharma Preface

Each ray of light is neither blue, yellow, red, white, nor black. They are neither form nor mind, neither existent nor nonexistent; they are dharmas of neither cause nor effect. They are the original source of the buddhas, the basis of the bodhisattvas, the basis for the disciples of the Buddha who fill the great assembly. Therefore the disciples of the Buddha in the great assembly should receive and maintain, read and recite, and study [the precepts] well.

The Preface for the Disciples

Disciples of the Buddha, listen well! If you receive the Buddha's precepts, whether you are a king or a prince, a major official or a minister, a *bhikṣu* or a *bhikṣuṇī,* if you are beings in the eighteen Brahmā heavens, or *deva* children in the six heavens of the desire realm, or common people or eunuchs, debauched men, prostitutes, or menials, or one of the eight kinds of spiritual beings, *vajra* spirits, animals, or magically conjured persons—by simply understanding the words of the Dharma teacher, fully accepting the precepts, all of you are called "the most pure."

The Main Sermon

The Buddha addressed his disciples:

There are ten grave *Prātimokṣa*s. If you receive the bodhisattva precepts but do not recite them, you are not a bodhisattva, nor do you have the seed of the Buddha. I also recite them.

Introduction of the Exhortation to Uphold

All [past] bodhisattvas have already studied these precepts, all [future] bodhisattvas will study these precepts, and all bodhisattvas [of the present] are now studying these precepts. I have already explained the features of the bodhisattva *Prātimokṣa.* You should study and, with a reverent mind, uphold and observe them.

The Ten Grave Precepts

1. Prohibition of Killing for Pleasure

The Buddha said:

> My disciples, if you yourself kill, or you incite someone else to kill, or you participate in the planning of a killing, or praise killing, or enjoy seeing someone kill, or kill by magical spells, then you have the causes of killing, the conditions of killing, the method of killing, the act of killing; this holds true even for the accidental killing[20] of any form of life. Bodhisattvas should give rise to an enduring attitude of compassion, an attitude of reverence and obedience, and devise skillful means to save and protect all sentient beings. On the other hand, if a bodhisattva kills a living creature and takes pleasure in the act, this constitutes a bodhisattva *pārājika* offense.

2. Prohibition of Stealing Others' Property

> My disciples, you should not yourself steal, incite others to steal, or steal through deception; if you engage in the causes of stealing, the conditions of stealing, the planning of stealing, the act of stealing, or stealing through magical spells, and so on, up to stealing the property of spiritual beings or the property of thieves—no matter what object is stolen, whether a single needle or blade of grass, or even if you have stolen by accident. A bodhisattva generates the buddha-nature mind of reverence and compassion, always assisting all people to bring about well-being and happiness. If instead you steal others' wealth and possessions, this is a *pārājika* offense for bodhisattvas.

3. Prohibition of the Heartless Pursuit of Lust

> My disciples, you should not engage in lustful behavior, incite someone to engage in lustful behavior, or even indulge in unplanned lustful behavior with any woman; you should avoid the causes of debauchery, the conditions of lustful behavior, the planning of lustful behavior, and the consummated act of lustful behavior. This includes everything up to sexual gratification with female animals, female celestials, or female spirits, as well as deviant forms of sexual conduct.[21] Moreover, bodhisattvas should

give rise to an attitude of piety; they should save all sentient beings by providing them with the pure teaching. If instead they repeatedly indulge in lustful behavior with anyone, engaging in sexual acts with animals, 1004c or one's mother, daughter, sister, or another close relative,[22] then this is cruelty and constitutes a bodhisattva *pārājika* offense.

4. Prohibition of Intentional Lying

My disciples, if you engage in lying on your own, encourage others to lie, or lie through deception, then you are involved in the causes of lying, the conditions of lying, the method of lying, and the act of lying. This also includes saying that one has seen what one has not seen, saying you have not seen something that you have seen, or lying [implicitly] through bodily actions or within one's own mind. Bodhisattvas always give rise to right speech and right views, and also lead all sentient beings to practice right speech and right views. If, on the other hand, you lead sentient beings to wrong speech, wrong views, and wrong activities, this constitutes a bodhisattva *pārājika* offense.

5. Prohibition of the Sale of Alcohol

My disciples, if you yourself sell alcohol, or you encourage others to do so, then herein are the causes of selling alcohol, the conditions for selling alcohol, the method of selling alcohol, and the act of selling alcohol. All kinds of alcohol should not be sold, as [consumption of alcohol] leads to the commission of [other] crimes. Instead, bodhisattvas should give rise to penetrating wisdom in all sentient beings. If, on the other hand, they lead sentient beings into distorted states of mind [by selling them alcohol], this is a bodhisattva *pārājika* offense.

6. Prohibition of Speaking of the Faults of Others

My disciples, if you yoursef speak about the faults of renunciant bodhi-sattvas, lay bodhisattvas, *bhikṣu*s, *bhikṣuṇī*s, or you encourage someone else to speak of their faults, then you have enacted the causes of fault-finding, the conditions of fault-finding, the method of fault-finding, and the act of fault-finding. When bodhisattvas hear about non-Buddhists or evil adherents of the two vehicles who talk about that within the buddha-dharma which is not the Dharma and not the Vinaya, they should always be compassionate. They should teach these unwholesome adherents and cause them to give rise to wholesome faith in the Great Vehicle. If instead bodhisattvas discuss the faults of those within the fold of the buddha-dharma, this is a bodhisattva *pārājika* offense.

7. Prohibition of Praising Oneself and Disparaging Others

My disciples, if with your own mouth you praise yourself and disparage others, or if you encourage people to praise themselves and disparage others, then you have the causes of disparagement of others, the conditions of disparagement of others, the method of disparagement of others, and the act of disparagement of others. On behalf of sentient beings, bodhisattvas should receive their blame and reflect on their own wrongdoings, and attribute good works to others. If you proclaim your own merits and cover up other people's good works, causing them to be disparaged, this constitutes a bodhisattva *pārājika* offense.

8. Prohibition of Parsimony and Abuse of Others

My disciples, if you yourself are stingy, or you encourage others to be stingy, then you have carried out the causes of parsimony, the conditions of parsimony, the methods of parsimony, and the act of parsimony. When seeing any destitute person begging for help, a bodhisattva should offer whatever that person needs. But if a bodhisattva in a wicked and hateful state of mind does not offer so much as a single coin, a single needle, or a single blade of grass [to someone in need], or does not teach one phrase, one verse—not even a tiny grain of the Dharma for seekers of the Dharma—and instead humiliates that person, this constitutes a bodhisattva *pārājika* offense.

1005a

9. Prohibition of Holding Resentments and Not Accepting Apologies

My disciples, if you are hateful or encourage others to be hateful, then you have the causes of hatred, the conditions of hatred, the framework of hatred, and the activity of hatred. Instead, a bodhisattva should encourage the growth of wholesome roots in all sentient beings, and without quarreling always generate compassion. If instead you insult and revile sentient and non-sentient beings, or pummel them with your fists, or attack them with knives or sticks, and do not let up in your anger even when this person seeks reconciliation; if he or she approaches with sincere words of apology and you still do not release your anger, this constitutes a bodhisattva *pārājika* offense.

10. Prohibition of Denigration of the Three Treasures

If, my disciples, you denigrate the Three Treasures or encourage others to denigrate them, then you have the causes of denigration, the conditions of denigration, the form of denigration, and the action of denigration. Instead, if a bodhisattva hears a non-Buddhist or an evil person uttering even a single word of denigration of the Buddha, it should feel to that bodhisattva as if three hundred sharp spears were piercing his heart. How, then, could he himself slander [the Buddha] and not give rise to the mind of faith and a complaisant attitude? If instead he assists such evil people and those with mistaken views in slandering [the Three Treasures], then this constitutes a bodhisattva *pārājika* offense.

Conclusion

All good students: this is the ten-part *Prātimokṣa* of the bodhisattvas, which you should study. You should not break even one of these precepts, as if [violating] just one is not such a big issue—much less should you break all ten! If someone violates [the precepts] in this way, he will not attain the awakening of the mind of enlightenment in this lifetime; he will fail at kingship, he will fail at wheel-turning kingship; he or she will fail as a *bhikṣu* or *bhikṣuṇī;* he will fail at the practice of the ten stages of departure toward the destination, at the ten stages of nurturance, at the ten adamantine stages, at the ten grounds, and at the stage of the marvelous fruit of the ever-abiding buddha-nature. [Someone who violates these precepts] will fail at all of these and fall into the three evil destinies, and for a duration as long as two or three *kalpa*s he or she will not hear the name of his father or mother, or the Three Treasures. Therefore, you should avoid breaking any one of these precepts. All of you bodhisattvas who are now studying, who will study, and who have already studied these ten precepts should

study them with an attitude of reverence and uphold them. They are
explained in detail in the "Chapter on the Eighty Thousand Rules of
Conduct."

The Minor Precepts

The Buddha addressed the bodhisattvas, "Now that I have fully explained
the ten-part *Prātimokṣa* I will now explain the forty-eight minor precepts."

Division of Ten Precepts

Precepts Concerning the Guarding
of One's Own Thoughts

1. Do Not Show Disrespect to Senior Teachers

My disciples, if you want to become the king of a country, or a wheel-
turning king, or a government official, you should first accept the bodhisattva precepts. All the spirits will protect the bodies of kings and officials, and the buddhas will be pleased. Once you have received the
precepts you should give rise to a pious and reverent attitude. When
you see the head monk, your teacher, an *ācārya*,[23] or one who excels
in the same kind of learning, or one with the same views, or one carrying
out the same practice, you should rise to respectfully greet them, bow
deeply, and show obeisance to them. If, on the other hand, haughty,
proud, or foolish bodhisattvas do not rise up to greet and bow in reverence, every single offering is wrong, from the perspective of the
Dharma. [In this case,] you should sell your own body, countries, cities,
men, women, the seven precious metals, and all kinds of possessions
and offer these [to respected monks]. If you don't do this, then you
commit a minor transgression of the precepts.

1005b

2. Do Not Drink Alcohol

My disciples, if you intentionally drink alcohol, there is no limit to the
mistakes and violations you will make. If with your own hand you pass
the wine bottle to another, you will be born without hands for five hundred lifetimes—how much worse if you drink the wine yourself? You

should not encourage any person to drink, nor any sentient being to do so; how much worse if you yourself drink alcohol yourself? If you intentionally drink, or encourage someone else to do so, you have committed a minor transgression of the precepts.

Protecting Others' Mental Functions

3. Do Not Eat Meat

My disciples, you should not intentionally eat meat. The consumption of meat is entirely unacceptable, as doing so will cut you off from the seed-lineage of great compassion. Whenever sentient beings see you they will avoid you. Therefore, bodhisattvas cannot eat the flesh of sentient beings. To eat meat is to invite countless sins. Eating meat constitutes a minor transgression of the precepts.

4. Do Not Eat the Five Pungent Roots

My disciples, you should not eat the five pungent roots: garlic, scallion, leek, onion, and asafoetida. Food that contains any of these five aromatics should not be eaten. If you intentionally eat any of these, you have committed a minor transgression of the precepts.

5. Do Not Fail to Encourage Others to Repent

My disciples, if you see any sentient beings violating the eight precepts,[24] the five precepts,[25] or the ten precepts,[26] or who are defying the prohibitions by way of the seven heinous acts[27] or the eight difficult circumstances,[28] or any other kind of violation of the precepts, you should encourage them to repent. If a bodhisattva does not encourage [a transgressor] to repent and continues to live together with them in the same beneficial circumstances of the sangha, or participate in the same repentance sessions, or the whole group recites the precepts together yet they fail to reveal their sins and they do not encourage [the transgressor] to repent their crimes in some part, this is a minor transgression of the precepts.

Revering and Cultivating
the Buddha-dharma

6. Do Not Fail to Request Instruction in the Dharma from Visiting Teachers

If, my disciples, you see a Dharma teacher of the Great Vehicle, or a fellow student who has the same views and does the same Great Vehicle practices, and he enters the monastery, a house, or the city—whether he has come from a distance of one hundred or one thousand *li*,[29] you should rise up to greet him and to send him off, bowing deeply and making offerings. You should make offerings three times a day, every day, providing daily food equal in value to three *liang* of gold. You should offer tasty food and drink, as well as bedding and medicine. You should serve this Dharma teacher with whatever he needs and provide anything that he requires. You should always request that he lecture on the Dharma three times a day, and you should pay obeisance to him three times every day, without any anger or anxiety. You should offer yourself fully for the Dharma, seeking it without laziness. If you do not do this you have committed a minor transgression of the precepts.

These ten precepts should be studied with reverence and upheld. They are explained in detail in the following six chapters.

7. Do Not Miss a Chance to Attend Dharma Lectures

My disciples, the Vinaya scripture is lectured on everywhere. When a large house is the venue for a Dharma lecture, newly awakened bodhisattvas should bring their sutra and vinaya scrolls and go to the place of that Dharma teacher to listen and ask questions. Whether the venue is under the trees in the forest, or in a room owned by the sangha, or any other place, you should listen to the best of your ability. If you fail to attend such a lecture, this constitutes a minor transgression of the precepts.

1005c

8. Do Not Abandon the Great Vehicle and Regress to the Lesser Vehicle

My disciples, if you turn away from the eternally abiding scriptures and the moral code of the Great Vehicle, declaring that these are not the Buddhist teachings, and instead you accept and maintain the wrong views of adherents of the two vehicles or non-Buddhists, along with all of their prohibitions and scriptures and moral discipline based on mistaken views, then you have committed a minor transgression of the precepts.

**Saving and Protecting
Sentient beings**

9. Do Not Fail to Care for the Ill

My disciples, if you see someone who is ill, you should always make offerings to them, no differently than you would for the Buddha. Among the eight fields of merit, that of caring for the ill is foremost. If your father or mother, teacher, fellow monk, or disciple is ill, handicapped, or suffering from any kind of ailment, he or she should be cared for until their illness is removed. If, however, bodhisattvas with a sense of malice see an ill person in the confines of the monastery, in the city, in an open field, or on a forest pathway and they do not help that ailing person, this is a minor transgression of the precepts.

10. Do Not Amass Weapons

My disciples, you should not amass weapons such as knives, clubs, bows and arrows, halberds, or axes; all evil instruments that are used to ensnare and kill living beings should not be collected. Since bodhisattvas cannot take revenge even for the killing of their father or mother, how could they possibly take the life of any sentient being? If one intentionally stores knives and clubs, this constitutes a minor transgression of the precepts.

Division of Ten Precepts

[The following ten precepts are divided into two groups. The first four deal with protecting one's own virtue. The latter six deal with protecting and gathering in others.]

Guarding One's Own Virtue

11. Do Not Serve as a Negotiator for the Military

The Buddha said:

> My disciples, you should not serve as an emissary to a foreign state for self-gain or with evil intentions when it involves raising armies to engage in battle and kill countless sentient beings. Bodhisattvas should not be involved in military matters at all—how much worse it would be to turn traitor to one's own country! If you intentionally do such a thing, this constitutes a minor transgression of the precepts.

12. Do Not Get Involved in Trade and Business that Causes Trouble for Others

> My disciples, you should not intentionally engage in buying and selling people, slaves, or the six kinds of animals. Nor should you engage in the trade of wood for constructing coffins for the dead. Since you should not engage in such activities yourself, how much more so should you not encourage others to engage in such activities. If you intentionally engage in these activities or encourage others to do so, this constitutes a minor transgression of the precepts.

1006a

13. Do Not Make Groundless Accusations

> My disciples, you should not maliciously and groundlessly accuse upright people, wholesome people, Dharma teachers, revered monks, kings, or nobles, saying that they have committed one of the seven heinous acts or one of the ten grave transgressions. You should have filial piety and compassion toward your parents, siblings, and the rest of the six kinds of relatives. If instead you cause them extreme harm, or accuse them of having committed a *pārājika* offense, this constitutes a minor violation of the precepts.

14. Do Not Harm Living Beings by Setting Fires

> My disciples, you should not out of evil intent set large fires in the forests and fields, or set fires from the fourth through the ninth months; nor should you set fire to others' homes, towns, monastic quarters, gardens

and groves, nor should you burn up spiritual implements or public property. No one's property should be set afire. If you intentionally set fires in this way, this constitutes a minor transgression of the precepts.

Bringing Others into the Fold
and Protecting Them

15. Do Not Teach Non-Buddhist Doctrines

My disciples, toward other disciples, non-Buddhists, evil persons, all your relatives, all your good comrades—in each case you should always teach them to follow and uphold the scriptures and rules of discipline of the Great Vehicle. You should teach them so that they understand the meaning, and cause them to give rise to the aspiration for enlightenment, the ten departures toward the destination, the ten kinds of nourishing mental states, the ten adamantine mental states, and, within each of these thirty mental states, to understand the order and application of the teachings. If instead a bodhisattva, out of wickedness or ill-will, wrongly teaches the sutras and vinaya of the two vehicles or of *śrāvaka*s, or the mistaken theories of non-Buddhists, then this constitutes a minor transgression of the precepts.

16. Do Not be Parsimonious with Offering Material Wealth or the Dharma

My disciples, you should, with a proper attitude, first study the Great Vehicle protocols of behavior, scriptures, and moral code, and broadly clarify their meanings. Later, if you encounter a newly initiated bodhisattva who has come from as far away as a hundred or a thousand *li* seeking the Great Vehicle scriptures or vinaya, you should explain according to Buddhist doctrine all the arduous practices, such as burning the body, the arm, or the fingers. If the newly initiated bodhisattva refuses to burn his body, arms, or fingers as offerings to the buddhas, he is not a renunciant bodhisattva. You should fully offer your body to hungry tigers, wolves, and lions, as well as to all hungry ghosts, including the flesh from your arms and legs. After you have done this, you should expound the correct Dharma for them in an orderly way, allowing their minds to open so that they may understand the meaning. If a bodhisattva, focused on their personal own gain, does not answer what should be answered, or if he or she elucidates the sutras and vinaya in a confused way, citing passages in no particular order, or if they offer a teaching that denigrates the Three Treasures, this constitutes a minor transgression of the precepts.

17. Do Not Seek to Gain Political Influence

My disciples, do not seek to be intimate with kings, princes, high ministers, or government officials in order to secure food and drink, money, profit, or fame for yourself. Nor should a bodhisattva expect to gain attention, beg for alms, strike or beat anyone, drag matters in unfair directions, or grab for money and possessions. All kinds of profit-seeking are called wrong hankering, voracious hankering, and inducing others to seek personal gain. A bodhisattva who does such acts, completely lacking compassion or piety, commits a minor transgression of the precepts.

18. Do Not Pretend to Be An Accomplished Teacher

1006b My disciples, you should deeply study and recite the moral code and memorize the bodhisattva precepts throughout the six divisions of the day and night, in order to understand their inner principle, which is the essence of buddha-nature. If a bodhisattva does not understand the causes and conditions of a single passage or a single verse of the moral code yet falsely claims that he does, he is [guilty of] deceiving himself as well as others. If you understand nothing of the Dharma, yet play the role of preceptor and impart the precepts, this amounts to a minor transgression of the precepts.

19. Do Not Get Involved in Treachery

My disciples, when you see monks who are observing the precepts, holding censers, and engaged in bodhisattva practices, you should not maliciously initiate disputes between them. If you disparage and deceive worthy people there is no evil you will not do. This is considered a minor transgression of the precepts.

20. Do Not Fail to Help Both the Living and the Deceased

My disciples, you should compassionately engage in the practice of releasing captive animals into the wild. All men have been our fathers, and all women our mothers. In our numerous past lives there is no one who has not been our mother or father. Therefore, sentient beings in all six destinies have all been our fathers and mothers. If we were to slaughter and eat them, it would be the same as slaughtering and eating our own parents, as well as slaughtering [and eating] my own former body. All lands and waters are my former body; all fire and wind are my original essence. Therefore you should always carry out freeing captive animals so that living beings can continue to be reborn and undergo rebirth. The eternally abiding Dharma encourages people to free living beings. When you see someone in society killing animals, you should try to come up with a way to protect the creatures and release them from their predicament. Always teaching through lecturing on the bodhisattva's moral code, you save sentient beings.

On the day of the death of your father, mother, or elder or younger siblings you should request a Dharma teacher to deliver a lecture from the *Bodhisattva Vinaya Sutra* in order to convey blessings on the deceased that they may attain a vision of the buddhas and be reborn as a human being or as a celestial. If you fail to do this, you are committing a minor transgression of the precepts.

You should study the above ten precepts (i.e., items 11–20), and uphold them with reverence. Each is explained in detail in the "Chapter on Expiating Sins."

[Conclusion of the second set of ten precepts]

Division of Ten Precepts

[The below ten precepts give form to the six ways that allow Buddhist practitioners to live in harmony. They are divided up according to theme into groups of three, one, four, and two, respectively. These categories are based on common activities, benefits, and precepts. Since the first three have in common the three karmic activities, they give form to the six ways that allow practitioners to live in harmony.]

The Shared Cultivation of the
Three Karmic Activities

21. Do Not Be Intolerant of Wrongs Done by Others
The Buddha said:

> My disciples, you should not repay anger with anger or violence with violence. Even if someone were to murder your parents, siblings, or other family members, you should not take revenge. Nor should you seek vengeance if the ruler or king of your country is murdered. Taking life and exacting retribution for the taking of life are not the way of respectful piety. One should not even keep servants, or abuse and revile others. Among the three karmic activities (i.e., acts of body, speech, and mind) that are carried out daily, verbal crimes are countless. How could you deliberately carry out the seven heinous acts? Yet if a renunciant bodhisattva retaliates without compassion—even for harm done to a member of their family—such intentional retaliation constitutes a minor transgression of the precepts.

22. Do Not Arrogantly Despise Your Dharma Teacher

> My disciples, suppose that when you have first renounced the world but have not yet attained any realization you feel proud of your intelligence and knowledge, or perhaps you presume upon your high social status or seniority, or perhaps you presume upon on your family's influence or wealth, your great advantage and merit, your possession of wealth and the seven precious metals. You should not, out of pride based on these things, fail to openly receive instruction on the scriptures and vinayas from learned Dharma teachers. A Dharma teacher may be from a minor family, or younger, or from a humble background, or extremely poor, or even handicapped, yet he may truly possess virtue and have fully digested all the scriptures and vinayas. Newly initiated bodhisattvas should not concern themselves with a Dharma teacher's family background. If you do not openly receive the cardinal truth taught by [a qualified] Dharma teacher, you have committed a minor transgression of the precepts.

1006c

23. Do Not Despise Beginning Practitioners

My disciples, if after my passing you wish with a sincere mind to receive
the bodhisattva precepts, you should take the vows on your own before
an image of a buddha or bodhisattva. You should practice repentance in
front of the buddha image for a week, and once you have experienced
an auspicious vision you will receive the precepts. If you are unable
to obtain a vision of the buddha's or bodhisattva's marks, you should
continue this practice for two weeks, three weeks, even up to a whole
year, until you obtain a vision of the marks. Once you have obtained
the vision you can immediately accept the precepts in front of the image
of the buddha or bodhisattva. If you do not have this vision, even if
you have accepted the precepts in front of the image you have not actu-
ally attained them. In any case, when you accept the precepts in the
presence of a Dharma teacher, it is not necessary to have a vision of
an auspicious sign. Why? Because the Dharma teachers have passed
the precepts down to one another, teacher to teacher, and for this reason
an auspicious vision [of the marks] is not necessary. Therefore, when
you accept the precepts in the presence of a Dharma teacher, all you
need in order to properly attain them is an attitude of deep sincerity.
If there is no qualified preceptor within a thousand *li* you can take the
vows on your own before an image of a buddha or bodhisattva, but
you must subsequently receive [a vision of] an auspicious sign.

Suppose there is a Dharma teacher who is well versed in the sutras
and vinayas and has disciplined himself in the Great Vehicle, and
who has come to be regarded as a spiritual counselor by kings, princes,
and government officials. If such a Dharma teacher, when approached
with a question regarding the interpretation of the scriptures or vinayas
by a beginner bodhisattva, adopts an attitude of disdain, meanness,
or arrogance and does not sincerely answer the questions put to him,
one at a time, then he has committed a minor transgression of the
precepts.

Practicing with Those Who
Hold the Same Views

24. Do Not Fear the Superior and Follow the Inferior

My disciples, if you are in possession of the Buddha's scriptures and vinaya and the Dharma of the Great Vehicle, and as well possess the correct view, the true nature, and the true Dharma body, yet you do not apply yourself in practice, this is like owning the seven precious metals but tossing them away. Furthermore, if you apply yourself to mistaken views, the practices of the two vehicles or of non-Buddhists, secular classics, the various Abhidharma treatises, or works of literature, such practices will cut off buddha-nature and obstruct the causes and conditions of the path. This is not the practice of the bodhisattva path. If you intentionally do these things, this counts as a minor transgression of the precepts.

Properly Maintaining
the Sangha

25. Do Not Fail to Properly Fulfill Administrative Duties

My disciples, if after my demise you are put in charge of Dharma lectures, or of administering the Dharma, or of the monastic quarters, or of instruction, or of meditation sessions, or of the monks' travels, you should compassionately and skillfully resolve any squabbles that may 1007a arise. You should skillfully handle the property of the Three Treasures, making sure that there is nothing that is not used in its proper capacity, as if these items were your own possessions. If instead you disrupt the sangha, engage in conflict with others, or selfishly use the property of the Three Treasures, you have committed a minor transgression of the precepts.

26. Do Not Receive Guests Improperly

My disciples, if as a resident of a monastery you encounter a visiting bodhisattva monk who has come to stay in the monastery quarters or the guest quarters established by the king, or who has joined the summer meditation retreat or the large assembly, a resident monk should go to welcome him when he arrives and see him off when he leaves. You should provide him with food and drink, shelter, bedding, furniture, and various other necessities. If you have no material goods to offer you should put yourself and others out for hire [for jobs] in order to provide all that is necessary. If there is a donor who invites sangha members [to his home for a meal], the guest monk should also be given a fair share and the rector should distribute the invitation to the guest monk within the framework of standard protocol. If a former resident monk keeps such an invitation to himself and does not pass it on to the guest monk, that rector invites numberless sins. He is no different from an animal; he is not a monk and is not of Śākyamuni's lineage. If one deliberately acts in this way, this constitutes a minor transgression of the precepts.

27. Do Not Accept Personal Invitations

My disciples, none of you should accept personal invitations, or take offerings for yourselves. These kinds of offerings belong to the entire sangha, so when you accept a personal invitation it means that you are appropriating the property of all the monks in the entire sangha and taking it as your own. To use the eight fields of merit, including buddhas, sages, the various kinds of monks and preceptors, one's father and mother, and those who are ill, for one's own purposes constitutes a minor transgression of the precepts.

28. Do Not Extend Personal Invitations to Monks

My disciples, if there is a renunciant bodhisattva, a householder bodhisattva, or a patron who wishes to invite a monk in order to gain merit, then at the time of making the invitation he should go to the monastery and speak to a monastery officer, saying, "I now wish [to make a request to invite a monk," to which the officer should respond,] "Invitations are distributed in order of seniority, which means that you will be gaining access to all enlightened monks in the monastery." Even though, [as recounted in some scriptures,] secular people gave private invitations to the five hundred arhats and bodhisattva monks, this is not as good as following the protocol of seniority and you may end up with an unenlightened monk. Giving personal invitations to monks is a custom of non-Buddhists. In the tradition of the Seven Buddhas there is no such custom as giving personal invitations, and it does not accord with the way of filial piety. If you intentionally make an invitation to a monk, this constitutes a minor transgression of the precepts.

Harmonizing and Polishing
the Precepts

29. Do Not Engage in Improper Livelihood

My disciples, you should not, with evil intent or in order to make profit, engage in selling sexual favors to men or women; you should not prepare food directly, touching it with your own hands, nor should you engage in grinding and milling [grain]. You should not practice divination to determine the compatibility of couples for marriage. You should not interpret dreams, practice fortune-telling, or predict the gender of an unborn child. You should not engage in sorcery, hired labor, or falconry; you should not concoct any of the hundred medicinal and poisonous herbs or the thousand kinds of venomous poisons and their antidotes; you should not engage in the production of gold and silver, or of bane. All [these acts] are conducive to cruelty, so if you deliberately do any of these sorts of things, this constitutes a minor transgression of the precepts.

30. Do Not Hurt People While Feigning Intimacy with Them

My disciples, if with bad intentions you denigrate the Three Treasures on your own, draw close to powerful people through pretense, glibly speak of emptiness while clinging to existence in your actions; serve as a go-between among secular people, or even as a matchmaker for couples, while you yourself are addicted to lust; and on the six days of purification or during the three long periods of purification you break the precepts by killing, stealing, and eating whenever you wish, then you have committed a minor transgression of the precepts.

1007b

You should study the above ten precepts (i.e., items 21–30) and uphold them with reverence. Their detailed exegesis is contained in the "Chapter on Regulations and Precepts."

Division of Nine Precepts

[The following nine precepts deal with initiating correct activities (giving), suppressing distractions, avoiding harmful influences, keeping oriented toward the correct vehicle, establishing and wearing vows, avoiding danger and disorder, always bringing benefit and joy.]

Making Proper Donations

31. Do Not Be Lax in Rescuing Vulnerable Articles and People from Danger

The Buddha said:

My disciples, in the evil world after my demise you may see non-Buddhists, evil people, or thieves selling images of buddhas and bodhisattvas, or of one's parents; or they may buy and sell sutras and vinayas, or buy and sell religious practitioners, including monks, nuns, and bodhisattvas who have given rise to the aspiration for enlightenment. Some venerable ones may be forced into government service, or become slaves to serve people. If a bodhisattva sees these kinds of goings-on he should compassionately endeavor to devise ways to rescue those [who are caught up in them]. He should teach people everywhere to retrieve things and restore images, and to redeem monks, nuns, and bodhisattvas who have given rise to the aspiration [for enlightenment] and preserve all vinayas and scriptures. If you do not rescue these [people and things], you have committed a minor transgression of the precepts.

Not Doing As One Pleases

32. Do Not Deviously Confiscate Others' Property

My disciples, you should not build up a store of swords, staves, or bows and arrows. You should not buy and sell goods using rigged scales and other means of measurement; you should not confiscate people's property using official authority, or maliciously tie people up, or sabotage their accomplishments. You should not raise cats, badgers, swine, or dogs. To intentionally do so constitutes a minor transgression of the precepts.

Avoiding Harmful Influences

33. Do Not Pass Your Time in Idleness

My disciples, you should not, with wrong intentions, be a spectator of quarrels between men and women, military battles, or brawls among gangsters. You should also not listen to the blowing of the conch, the beating of drums, or the horns [sounded when armies go into battle], nor [should you listen to] the music of guitars, harps, flutes, or lutes, nor to the singing and musical accompaniment in theatrical performances. You should not gamble with dice, nor play [such games as] checkers, chess, *danqi*,[30] Parcheesi, or cone-tossing, rock-tossing, or jar-tossing, or the game of "eight roads to the capital." You should not practice fortune-telling using the fingernail mirror, grass, willow twigs, bowls, or phrenology. You should also not serve as an accomplice for thieves. You should not do any of these things. If you do so intentionally, this counts as a minor transgression of the precepts.

Advancing in the
True Vehicle

34. Do Not Abandon the Aspiration for Enlightenment

My disciples, you should uphold the precepts when walking, standing, sitting, or lying down. You should chant these precepts throughout the six periods of the day and night. You should be as firm as adamant; as fervent as someone carrying a life raft who intends to cross the ocean; as morally upright as the monk tied up by the grass.[31] Always produce wholesome faith in the Great Vehicle and know yourself to be an incomplete buddha, while the buddhas are complete buddhas. Give rise to the aspiration for enlightenment and never abandon this aspiration, even for a moment. If you give rise to even one thought of following the practices of the two vehicles or of non-Buddhists, this constitutes a minor transgression of the precepts.

Not Avoiding Making
Vows

35. Do Not Fail to Make Vows

My disciples, you should always make vows to be filial and complaisant toward parents, teachers, monks, and the Three Treasures. You should vow to meet good teachers, fellow students, and other reliable Buddhist friends. You should vow to always teach my Great Vehicle scriptures and vinayas, the ten departures toward the destination, the ten kinds of nourishing [mental states], the ten adamantine mental states, and the ten grounds, making my teachings clear for others. You should vow to practice   1007c according to the Buddha's teachings, to firmly maintain the Buddha's moral code, even to the point of sacrificing your body and life, and never forget your vows for even a moment. If a bodhisattva does not give rise to these vows, this constitutes a minor transgression of the precepts.

Making Vows

36. Do Not Fail to Initiate Vows on Your Own

My disciples, once you have committed yourself to the ten great vows you will uphold the Buddha's precepts. You should vow, "I would rather throw my body into a raging fire or a great pit, or on top of a pile of swords than violate the buddhas' vinaya scripture throughout the three periods of time; I vow to never commit an immoral act with any woman."

You should also vow, "I would rather wrap myself in a net of burning steel of a thousand layers than with a body that has broken precepts regarding bodily actions ever accept any offerings of clothing from faithful donors."

You should also vow, "I would rather with my own mouth swallow hot iron balls, or even a great molten flow for a hundred thousand *kalpas*, than with a mouth that has broken the precepts verbally partake of any of the range of offerings of food and drink offered by faithful donors."

You should also vow, "I would rather, with my own body, lie down on ground that is covered with a great fiery net and red-hot swords, than with a body that has broken the precepts regarding bodily actions accept any of the wide varieties of seats or stools offered by faithful donors."

You should also vow, "I would rather have my own body be impaled by three hundred spears for one or two *kalpa*s, than with a body that has broken the precepts regarding bodily actions receive any of the wide varieties of medicine offered by faithful donors."

You should also vow, "I would rather my own body be thrown into a scorching iron cauldron and boiled for a hundred thousand *kalpa*s, than with a body that has broken the precepts regarding bodily actions receive any of the wide varieties of dormitory rooms, homes, groves, or farmland offered by faithful donors."

You should also vow, "I would rather have my body pulverized into dust by being beaten with iron mallets from head to toe, than with a body that has broken the precepts regarding bodily actions accept any forms of demonstration of reverence offered by faithful donors."

1008a

You should also vow, "I would rather have my own eyes gouged out by a hundred thousand red-hot iron swords, than with a mind that has broken the precepts regarding thoughts look upon the attractive form of another person [with desire]."

You should also vow, "I would rather have my ears pierced through with needles driven by a hundred thousand iron hammers for one or two *kalpa*s, than with a mind that has broken the precepts regarding thoughts listen to enjoyable music."

You should also vow, "I would rather have my nose cut off by a hundred thousand knives and swords, than with a mind that has broken the precepts regarding thoughts desire to savor various [pleasing] aromas."

You should also vow, "I would rather have my tongue cut off by a hundred thousand knives and swords, than with a mind that has broken the precepts regarding thoughts partake in the variety of delicious pure foods prepared by [donors]."

You should also vow, "I would rather have my body chopped up by sharp axes, than with a mind that has broken the precepts regarding thoughts desire to touch things to receive pleasant sensations."

You should also vow, "I vow to help all sentient beings, without exception, to attain enlightenment."

If bodhisattvas do not undertake these vows, this constitutes a minor transgression of the precepts.

Avoiding Danger

37. Do Not Intentionally Go to Dangerous Places

My disciples, you should always practice austerities (*dhūta*) at the two designated times, in the winter and summer intensive meditation training periods. When you go to the summer retreat you should bring your monastic requisites: willow twigs (for use as a toothbrush), soap, the three garments (robes), a water container, a bowl, a meditation mat, a walking staff, a censer, a water filter, a hand towel, a knife, a flintstone, tweezers, a folding seat, sutras, vinayas, a buddha image, and a bodhisattva image. When bodhisattvas practice austerities or when they travel, whether for a hundred or a thousand *li*, they should always have these eighteen articles with them. *Dhūta* should be practiced from the fifteenth of the first month up to the fifteenth of the third month, and from the fifteenth of the eighth month up to the fifteenth of the tenth month. A monk should always have these eighteen articles on his person during both of these periods, just as a bird always has its two wings.

On the days of *poṣadha* (precepts confession), the newly initiated bodhisattva monks will do *poṣadha* in biweekly installments. When they chant the ten grave and forty-eight minor precepts, they should offer their confession before images of the buddhas and bodhisattvas. If there is only one person doing *poṣadha,* there should be one person chanting. If there are two, three, or even a hundred thousand people doing *poṣadha,* there should also be one person chanting. The reciter should sit on the high seat with the listeners sitting below, each dressed in either a nine-panel, seven-panel, or five-panel robe. At the commencement of the summer retreat, each item of protocol should be followed according to the rules. When intensive discipline is being practiced, you should not enter dangerous places. You should not go into countries that are in political turmoil or ruled by evil kings. You should not enter precipitous areas, dense forests, or places where there are lions, tigers, or wolves. You should not enter places where there are floods, fires, or typhoons, or where there are brigands, nor should you walk on snake-infested paths. You should not enter such places in any case, but even more so should you not enter such places during a period of intensive discipline or a meditation retreat. If you are aware that a place is dangerous and yet you still deliberately go there, this constitutes a minor transgression of the precepts.

Not Creating Confusion

38. Do Not Take Your Place Out of Order

1008b My disciples, you should sit in the proper order. Those who received the precepts earlier should sit up front, and those who received the precepts later should sit at the back. This is not a question of one's physical age. Whether you are a monk, nun, aristocrat, king, prince, eunuch, or slave, all of you should follow the order of ordination seniority, with those who received the precepts earlier sitting at the front, and those who received the precepts later sitting at the back. You should not act like non-Buddhist fools who have no order in their seating arrangements, whether they are older or younger or began practice sooner or later. That is the way of soldiers and slaves. In our Buddhist protocol the seniors sit at the front and the juniors sit at the back. If bodhisattvas do not take their places in the proper order, this constitutes a minor transgression of the precepts.

Profit and Happiness

39. Do Not Pursue Personal Gain

My disciples, you should always teach all sentient beings to construct monastic dwellings and to erect buddha stupas in the forests and fields. For the winter and summer meditation retreats they should set up places for meditation and all kinds of facilities for the cultivation of the Way. Bodhisattvas should lecture on the Great Vehicle vinayas and sutras for all sentient beings, even when they are ill, or when there is national instability, or when beset by brigands. On funeral days and on the twenty-first and forty-ninth days after the passing of parents, siblings, teachers, or preceptors, you should also chant and lecture on the Great Vehicle vinayas and sutras, praying for the merit [of those who have recently departed] at these assemblies. For the well-being of those who are traveling, those who are threatened by wildfires, those who are adrift at sea, those whose ships are tossed about in violent storms, those for whom the great rivers and seas are plagued by ogres—you should also chant and lecture on the vinayas and sutras. Also, for those who are incurring the three kinds of retribution for their past misdeeds, such as the seven heinous acts or the eight difficult circumstances; whose bodies are bound with cuffs, shackles, pillories, and waist chains; who have much lust, anger, and stupidity, and who suffer from disease—you should chant and lecture on the vinayas and sutras for all of them. If a newly initiated bodhisattva does not do this, it constitutes a minor transgression of the precepts.

Division of Nine Precepts

The following nine precepts should be studied earnestly and maintained reverently. They are explained in detail in the "Chapter on Brahmadaṇḍa."

[Among the following nine precepts, the first five deal with using moral discipline to gather believers, and the final four deal with the compassionate instruction offered to others. The first five are the container for reception, selecting and rejecting, guarding the external, guarding the internal, and being respectful. The final four are preaching to people and leading them, teaching and converting, suppressing evil, and protecting the correct.]

Using Moral Discipline
to Gather [Believers]

Gathering in People of Various Capacities

40. Do Not Err in Terms of Who Can Be Taught

The Buddha said:

My disciples, you should not discriminate when conferring the precepts on people. Whether they are kings, princes, senior ministers, or government officials; monks, nuns, male and female lay believers; libertines or prostitutes; whether they are the celestials of the eighteen Brahmā heavens, or the celestial children of the six heavens of desire; whether they are sexless or hermaphrodites, eunuchs or slaves, or disembodied spirits—all should be able to receive the precepts. Those who would confer the precepts should wear monastic garb, which should be of muted colors, appropriate for the religious path. [The monastic robes] should be dyed blue, yellow, red, black, or purple. All dyed garments, as well as all bedding, should be of muted color. Whatever garments are worn should be of muted dyed color. In whatever land you may be teaching in, there should be a difference between the clothes worn by monks and nuns and those of the secular people of that place.

1008c

When someone wishes to receive the precepts, the preceptor should inquire, "In this life, have you ever committed one of the seven heinous acts?" A bodhisattva preceptor should not confer the precepts on anyone who has committed one of the seven heinous acts in this life. The seven heinous acts are wounding a buddha, killing one's father or mother, killing one's teacher, killing one's preceptor, disrupting the sangha, and killing an arhat. If someone has committed any one of these seven heinous acts, he or she cannot receive the precepts in this lifetime. Anyone else can receive the precepts. Those who have renounced the world should not pay homage to kings or pay obeisance to their parents; they should not show special respect to any of their close relatives, and they should not sacrifice to departed spirits. Anyone who can understand a Dharma teacher's words, whether they come from as far as a hundred or a thousand *li* to seek the Dharma, may receive the precepts. If a bodhisattva Dharma teacher, with malice or anger, does not confer the precepts upon any [suitable] sentient being, this constitutes a minor transgression of the precepts.

Separating Out Wrong Situations

41. Do Not Seek Disciples for the Wrong Reasons

My disciples, when those whom you teach give rise to faith, you, bodhisattvas, and someone else should work together to instruct them in the precepts. If you see someone who wishes to receive the precepts, you should encourage him to engage two teachers, a senior teacher and a preceptor. These two teachers should ask him or her, "Have you ever committed any of the seven heinous acts?" If the person has committed any one of the seven heinous acts in this lifetime, the teachers should not confer the precepts; if he or she hasn't, then they can receive them. If [the one requesting precepts] has broken one of the ten precepts, you should teach him or her how to repent: they should go before an image of a buddha or bodhisattva and recite the ten grave and forty-eight minor precepts throughout the six periods of the day and night. They should then prostrate to the thousand buddhas of the three periods of time, seeking to receive an auspicious sign. If necessary, they can repeat this for one, two, or three weeks, up to an entire year, seeking an auspicious sign. An auspicious sign would be something like a buddha coming and touching their head, seeing halos, or other various types of marvelous signs. As soon as the sign is witnessed the sin is erased.

If no auspicious sign is forthcoming, no matter how much someone repents it is in vain. Such a person cannot in this life receive the bodhisattva precepts; but if he or she obtains and auspicious sign they can receive the precepts [in the future].[32] If one has transgressed one of the forty-eight minor precepts, they should make a face-to-face confession to their preceptors and the sin will be erased. This is different from the case of the seven heinous acts.

As a preceptor you must understand well every part of this process. You must understand the vinayas and sutras of the Great Vehicle, know what offenses are light and heavy, and what constitutes an offense and what does not; you must understand the cardinal truth, and the greater and lesser among these, entering and leaving the practice of clear obser-   1009a
vation and the ten limbs of meditation. If a bodhisattva does not grasp the inner point of every single type of practice but for personal profit or fame seeks to acquire students, either wrongly or excessively; or if in order to gain profit and disciples he or she misrepresents their grasp of vinaya scriptures in order to receive offerings, such a person only deceive themselves and others. If with such motivations a bodhisattva

confers the precepts on someone, this constitutes a minor transgression of the precepts.

Guarding the External

42. Do Not Give the Precepts to Unsuitable People

My disciples, you should not, with the intent of gaining some kind of personal advantage, discuss the Mahayana precepts of the thousand buddhas before those who have not yet received them, nor in front of evil non-Buddhists. You should also not discuss them before people who hold mistaken views. Except for kings, you should not discuss them with any other people. The evil people who do not receive the Buddhist precepts are called animals; lifetime after lifetime they never recognize the Three Treasures. Being bereft of thought, like a piece of wood or a stone, they are called "non-Buddhists." People with mistaken views are no different from blocks of wood. If a bodhisattva discusses the moral code of the Seven Buddhas before these types of people, this constitutes a minor transgression of the precepts.

Guarding the Internal

43. Do Not Intentionally Break the Holy Precepts

My disciples, if someone has thoughts of faith and enters the order, receiving the Buddha's true precepts, but then intentionally violates the holy precepts, he or she should not receive any offerings from temple supporters, nor should they walk on the king's lands, nor should they drink the king's water. The five thousand great spirits will always block their way, calling them a great thief. If such a person enters monastery buildings, or goes into towns or homes, the demons will sweep up his footprints, returning things to the way they were before. All the people of the world will curse him, "You are a thief in the midst of the buddha-dharma!" Sentient beings will avert their eyes, not wishing to even look at him. A disciple who violates the precepts is no different from an animal or a block of wood. If a bodhisattva intentionally violates the true precepts, this constitutes a minor transgression of the precepts.

Showing Respect

44. Do Not Fail to Revere the Sutras and Vinayas

My disciples, with one-pointedness [of mind] you should always maintain and recite the sutras and vinayas of the Great Vehicle, even if you must use your own skin as paper, your own blood as ink, your own marrow to mix the ink, or split apart your own bones to make brushes in order to copy the Buddha's Vinaya.[33] Tree bark, rice paper, undyed silk, and bamboo slats can also serve as media for writing. You should always use the seven precious metals, priceless incense and flowers, and all kinds of other jewels to adorn the containers for the sutra and vinaya scrolls. If a bodhisattva does not make offerings according to this kind of protocol, this constitutes a minor transgression of the precepts.

Teaching by Means of Compassion

Being Proactive

45. Do Not Fail to Teach Sentient Beings

My disciples, you should always give rise to an attitude of great compassion. When you go into into various towns and homes and encounter sentient beings you should exhort them, "You must all take refuge in the Three Treasures and accept the ten precepts." When you see any kind of animal, such as cattle, horses, swine, or sheep, you should think in your mind and say to them, "You animals should awaken the aspiration for enlightenment." When a bodhisattva goes out into the mountains, rivers, forests, and fields he or she should enable all sentient beings to awaken the aspiration for enlightenment. If a bodhisattva 1009b does not stimulate the minds of sentient beings and teach them, this constitutes a minor transgression of the precepts.

Teaching Others

46. Do Not Preach the Dharma Using Improper Protocol

My disciples, you should always teach people with a greatly compassionate attitude. Whether you are visiting aristocratic patrons or among a general crowd of people, you should not expound the Dharma for laypeople while standing but only while seated on a raised seat in front of them. *Bhikṣu* Dharma teachers should not stand on the ground while expounding the Dharma for the four groups of Buddhist believers. During the Dharma lecture a master's raised seat should be decorated with offerings of incense and flowers, and the four groups [of followers] should listen from their seats below. One should respect the teacher in the same way one shows filial piety to one's parents, or as the fire-worshiping brahmans do. If a Dharma lecture is not conducted in the proper way, this constitutes a minor transgression of the precepts.

Warding off Evil

47. Do Not Establish Systems that Undermine the Dharma

My disciples, you should all receive my precepts with an attitude of faith. There may be kings, princes, government officials, or members of the four groups of disciples who take pride in their high positions and seek to undermine my moral code and my Dharma. They may seek to revise the laws to restrict entry into the four groups of disciples, or attempt to prevent them from listening to the teachings of renunciant monks, or from listening to or printing the sutras and precepts, or from creating buddha images and building stupas. [They might also seek to establish government policies to regulate the sangha and establish an agency to oversee and register the monks. They would require bodhisattva monks to stand on the ground before their secular masters who sit on high seats, and to carry out widespread policies that are antithetical to Buddhist principles, forcing monks to serve them the way soldiers and slaves must serve their masters. Bodhisattvas should receive offerings from the people. If instead they are made to serve as errand boys for officials, this is contrary to the Dharma and the moral code. Kings and high officials should sincerely receive my precepts and not commit the offense of[34] despoiling the Three Treasures. If they deliberately undermine the Dharma, this constitutes a minor transgression of the precepts.

Maintaining Orthodoxy

48. Do Not Undermine the Dharma from Within

My disciples, you should enter the monastic order with utmost sincerity. You should not lecture on the precepts of the Seven Buddhas before kings and high officials merely for fame and profit, nor should you deviously initiate events that entangle *bhikṣus*, *bhikṣuṇīs*, and [lay] disciples who have received the bodhisattva precepts. This is like parasites that consume the flesh of a lion from within—[they may succeed in despoiling the Dharma] in a way that non-Buddhists and Devamāra could not. If a bodhisattva receives the Buddha's precepts, he or she should protect the Buddha's precepts, in just the same way a parent thinks of his only child, or as a child serves his parents. When a bodhisattva hears evil non-Buddhists denigrating the Buddha's precepts with foul language, it is just like three hundred spears piercing his heart, like a thousand swords and ten thousand clubs striking his body. "I would rather pass a hundred *kalpas* in hell than hear just once the sound of someone denigrating the Buddha's precepts in foul language." How much worse it is for someone to denigrate the precepts on his own, or try to create a situation in which someone else is encouraged to denigrate the Dharma? There is, indeed, no piety to be seen here. If a bodhisattva deliberately does this, it constitutes a minor transgression of the precepts.

You should study these nine precepts and uphold them with reverence. My disciples, you should memorize these forty-eight minor precepts. All bodhisattvas of the past have recited them, all bodhisattvas of the future will recite them, and all bodhisattvas of the present now recite them.

General Conclusion

My disciples, listen well! These ten grave and forty-eight minor precepts have been recited, will be recited, and are now being recited by the buddhas of the three periods of time; I also now recite them. All of those in the great assembly, whether you are kings, princes, high officials, monks, nuns, laymen, or laywomen, you who receive these bodhisattva precepts should memorize and recite them. You should explicate them, and copy them to make scrolls of the precepts of the ever-abiding buddha-nature, which should be transmitted through the three periods of time so that all sentient beings can be continually taught without interruption. Having gained a vision of the thousand buddhas, each buddha proffers his hand to you so that from lifetime to lifetime you will never fall into an evil rebirth or into the eight circumstances where it is difficult to encounter the Dharma. You will always be born as a human or celestial being.

I now sit beneath the *bodhi* tree and reveal in brief the teaching of the moral code of the Seven Buddhas. You should now, with full concentration, study the *Prātimokṣa* and practice it with joy and reverence. These [precepts] are all explained in detail, one by one, in the "Chapter on the Markless Heavenly King."

At that time, the three thousand monks who were sitting in the audience heard the Buddha recite the precepts himself. Their minds were filled with faith and, dancing with joy, they memorized these precepts.

Dissemination Section

Concluding Exhortation
for Faithful Practice

At that moment Śākyamuni Buddha finished his discourse on the "Chapter on the Dharma of the Ten Inexhaustible Precepts" from within the "Chapter on the Dharma Gate of the Mind-ground of Vairocana Buddha" in the world of the lotus flower platform store, as did millions of billions of Śākyamunis. They taught this in the ten locations, from the heavenly palace of Mahêśvara down to beneath the *bodhi* tree, for inexpressibly vast numbers of great assemblies of bodhisattvas, who have memorized, recited, and in turn explained the meaning of the content, just like this. In millions of billions of worlds, lotus store worlds, infinite numbers of worlds, all buddhas taught fully about all the stores of the buddha-mind, ground stores, precept stores, stores of immeasurable practices and vows, stores of the causes and effects of the eternally present buddha-nature, and the immeasurable store of all teachings. Within millions and billions of worlds, all sentient beings preserve these precepts, and joyfully receive and practice them. If we were to explain each aspect of the mind-ground in detail, it would be like that found in the "Chapter on Flower Radiance King Buddha."

> Bright people, whose tolerance and wisdom are strong
> Are able to uphold this Dharma.
> During the time when one has not [yet] attained enlightenment,
> One stably holds to five kinds of benefit.
> The first is the buddhas of the ten directions
> Who, with pity, always protect;
> The second is the direct vision of the mind of joy
> At the moment of death;
> Third is making friends with bodhisattvas
> In every rebirth;
> Fourth is that all merits,
> Such as the precepts and perfections, are complete;
> Fifth is that in present and future existences
> One's observance of natural law, merit, and wisdom is done to
>   its fullest.
> This sphere of activity of the buddhas
> Is something that the wise well consider.
> If you imagine a self and attach to marks,
> You cannot have faith in this teaching.
> Those who extinguish affliction and seize realization
> Are also not of an inferior type.
> Wishing to grow sprouts of *bodhi,*
> Your luminosity shines out upon the world.
> You should quietly contemplate
> The true character of dharmas,
> Which neither arise nor cease,
> Are neither eternal nor temporary,
> Neither the same nor different,
> Neither coming nor going.

Within this One Mind
There is the adornment by the application of skillful means.
The works of the bodhisattvas
Should be put into practice in order,
And you should not create thoughts of distinction
Between discipline and being beyond discipline.
This is called the Supreme Way—
It is all called the Mahayana.
All bases of intellectual play
Are fully extinguished from this point.
The omniscience of the buddhas
Is fully produced from this point.
Therefore, all Buddhist disciples
Should give rise to great courage.
They should guard the Buddha's pure precepts
Just as they would guard a bright gem.
The bodhisattvas of the past
Have already applied themselves at this.
Those of the future will also apply themselves,
And those of the present are now applying themselves [thus].
This field of buddha activities
Is extolled by the Holy Bhagavan.
Now, having explained accordingly,
The immeasurable heap of merit,
I return to sentient beings,
Together with the offering of omniscience.
Those who wish to hear this teaching
Will quickly attain the Buddha Way.

Notes

1   For a detailed discussion of this issue, see Tōru Funayama, "Bonmōkyō no shohon no ni keitō," *Toho gakuho Kyoto Daigaku Jinbun kagaku kenkyūsho* 80 (2010): 178–211, and "Bonmōkyō geken sengyo no sai kentō," in Kunio Mugitani, ed., *Sankyō kōshō ron zokuhen* (Kyoto: Kyōto Daigaku Jinbun Kagaku Kenkyūjo, 2011), pp. 127–156.

2   Charles Muller has published a full translation of this sutra along with Daehyeon's commentary, *The Collected Works of Korean Buddhism, Volume XI: Exposition of the Sutra of Brahmā's Net* (Seoul: Compilation Committee of Korean Buddhist Thought, Jogye Order of Korean Buddhism, 2012).

3   See Nobuyoshi Yamabe, "Visionary Repentance and Visionary Ordination In the Brahmā Net Sūtra," in William M. Bodiford, ed., *Going Forth: Visions of Buddhist Vinaya. Essays Presented in Honor of Professor Stanley Weinstein* (Honolulu: University of Hawai'i Press, 2005), pp. 17–39.

4   It is said that when Maitreya becomes a buddha 5.67 billion years hence, he will sit under the dragon-flower tree and preach at the dragon-flower assembly.

5   The ten powers (Skt. *daśa-balāni*) are kinds of powers of awareness specially possessed by the Buddha, which constitute perfect knowledge of (1) distinguishing right and wrong; (2) one's own karma, as well as the karma of every being in the past, present, and future; (3) all stages of *dhyāna* liberation and *samādhi;* (4) the relative capacities of sentient beings; (5) the desires or moral direction of every being; (6) the varieties of causal factors; (7) the range of courses and paths pursued by sentient beings; (8) remembrance of past lives; (9) where people will die and be reborn; and (10) the methods of destroying all evil afflictions.

6   The eighteen distinctive practices refers to the eighteen distinctive characteristics of the Buddha, which belong only to a buddha and not to *śrāvaka*s, *pratyeka-buddha*s, or bodhisattvas. In East Asian Buddhism these are (1) unmistaken action, (2) unmistaken word, (3) unmistaken mindfulness, (4) a mind of equality toward all beings, (5) a stable mind in meditation, (6) an all-embracing mind that rejects nothing, (7) the power of nonretrogression in terms of aspiration, (8) the power of nonretrogression in terms of diligence, (9) the power of nonretrogression in terms of mindfulness, (10) the power of nonretrogression in terms of wisdom toward the salvation of all beings, (11) the power of nonretrogression from freedom into bondage, (12) nonretrogression from the vision attained in liberation, (13) the manifestation of wisdom power in thought, (14) the manifestation of wisdom

power in word, (15) the manifestation of wisdom power in deed, (16) immediate total knowledge of all present affairs, (17) immediate total knowledge of all past affairs, and (18) immediate total knowledge of all future affairs. In Indian Buddhism these are the ten powers, the four kinds of fearlessness, the three bases of mindfulness, and great compassion.

[7] This line seems to be an abbreviation of one found in the *Mahayana Yoga of the Adamantine Ocean, Mañjuśrī with a Thousand Arms and Thousand Bowls: Great King of Tantras:* "For bodhisattvas who are in the state of mind of observing the precepts, the precepts are neither precepts nor non-precepts, lacking a recipient. In the ten wholesome precepts there is no teacher to expound the Dharma of the precepts, nor 'deception' and stealing, the same up to craving, ill-will, and wrong views" (T.1177a.20:760b28–c2).

[8] By context, as well as from the following commentary (where it is said to be the greatest harm that can be inflicted on a human being), it seems that the "crime of deception" is a scribal error for "killing." The only place the binome appears in scriptural sources in the entire Taishō canon is in the text cited in note 7, above, and in this text (and also in commentaries on these two works, through repeated citation). Lists of the objects of the ten precepts usually start with killing and stealing and proceed to wrong views.

[9] The eight inverted views are non-Buddhists' mistaken beliefs in permanence, happiness, self, and purity. The Hinayana asserts the opposite: impermanence, non-happiness, non-self, and impurity. The Mahayana denies these now but asserts them in nirvana.

[10] Thus, *satkāya-dṛṣṭi.*

[11] The eight difficulties or circumstances in which it is difficult to encounter a buddha or hear his teaching are: (1) the condition of a hell being, (2) of a hungry ghost, (3) or of an animal; (4) existence in the long-life heavens, where life is long and free of difficulty; (5) in Uttarakuru, the northern continent where all is pleasant; (6) as a deaf, blind, or mute person; (7) as a worldly philosopher; or (8) in the intermediate period between the passing of a buddha and the appearance of his successor.

[12] There are various definitions for the six kinds of familial relations. One representative set is comprised of one's parents, older and younger siblings, wife, and children.

[13] Lists of the seven holy assets (Skt. *saptāryadhāna*) vary slightly, according to the source. A representative list includes (1) faith, (2) moral discipline, (3) conscience, (4) shame, (5) hearing instruction or learning, (6) charity (used interchangeably with detachment), and (7) wisdom.

[14] I.e., understanding the emptiness of self and dharmas.

[15] This is also a name for the first of the mind-grounds.

[16] As a rendering of *duḥkha-duḥkha,* this is usually translated as "ordinary suffering," but in his commentary Daehyeon plays on the Chinese rendering of "suffering on top

of suffering." This means concrete suffering, physical suffering; the direct suffering that one experiences from illness, exhaustion, hunger, pain, etc. One of the three kinds of suffering.

17 In many cases the name Rocana is equivalent to Vairocana, but in some texts a distinction is made between Vairocana representing the Dharma body of the Buddha, and Rocana representing the enjoyment body or transformation body (*nirmāṇakāya*). See the entry "Ten Buddha Names" in the Digital Dictionary of Buddhism (http://www.buddhism-dict.net/ddb).

18 According to a better-known tradition, Gautama left home somewhat later, after being married. Thus other English translations render this as "after seven years as a world-renunciant" or something of that nature. That is not what this text has, however, and since Daehyeon makes note of this in his commentary, I render it as is.

19 *Prātimokṣa* literally means "liberation from all afflictions." In traditional vinaya discourse it usually refers to the body of precepts to be kept by monks and nuns, specifically a part of the Vinaya that contains the two hundred and twenty-seven disciplinary rules for monks and the three hundred and forty-eight rules for nuns that is recited at every *upoṣatha* (precepts confession) ceremony. In China the *Prātimokṣa* most often used was one associated with the vinaya of the Dharmaguptakas, which was rendered into Chinese as the *Four-part Vinaya* (*Sifen lü,* T. 1428). Over time, however, there were efforts in China to replace the "Hinayana" *Prātimokṣa* with a "Mahayana" one that could be used in rites of confession. This resulted in the development of the so-called bodhisattva precepts, which are the ten grave precepts of the *Brahmā's Net Sutra.*

20 Literally, killing "with unobtained reason," which Fazang glosses as "without harmful intention" (T.1813.40:613a29).

21 "Deviant sexual practices" means using bodily orifices other than the genitals, such as the mouth or anus, for sexual gratification. According to another explanation, this refers not only to using inappropriate bodily parts such as the mouth or anus, but also to having sexual relations at an inappropriate time, such as before and after a woman gives birth; in an inappropriate location, such as a cemetery or in view of people; to an inappropriate degree, such as excessive engagement in intercourse; and with inappropriate principles, such as going against societal values or mores.

22 See note 12 for the six familial relations.

23 A preceptor; originally, a master who taught Vedic rituals to disciples. In Indian Buddhism, the Sanskrit term *ācārya* means a teacher, master, or preceptor; an established monk who guides his students in conduct and sets an example; a spiritual teacher or master; one of correct conduct who is an examplar for others.

24 The eight precepts are the first eight of one interpretation of the ten precepts: (1) not to kill, not to take that which is not given, (3) not to engage in ignoble (i.e., sexual) conduct, (4) not to speak falsehoods, (5) not to ingest intoxicants, (6) not to indulge

in cosmetics, personal adornments, dancing, or music, (7) not to sleep on a high or luxurious bed (only on a mat on the ground), and (8) not to take food outside of the regulation hours, i.e., after noon. These are the eight precepts undertaken by laypeople six times per month, on the eighth, fourteenth, fifteenth, twenty-third, twenty-ninth, and thirtieth days according to the lunar calendar.

25 The five precepts (Skt. *pañca-śīla*) are the basic code of moral behavior to be observed by lay Buddhist householder-practitioners: (1) not killing, (2) not stealing, (3) not engaging in lustful behavior, (3) not using false speech, and (5) not ingesting intoxicants. These are binding on the laity, both male and female, as well as on monks and nuns. The observance of these five precepts ensures rebirth in the human realm.

26 The ten precepts are also the ten basic precepts for *bhikkhu*s (Skt. *bhikṣu*) and *bhikkhunī*s (Skt. *bhikṣunī*) in Theravāda and Nikāya Buddhism. The first five of these are the same five precepts observed by lay practitioners (see note 25), and additionally include proscriptions against eating after noon, attending performances of dancing, singing, and theater, adorning oneself with garlands, perfumes, and ointments, using a high bed, and receiving gold and silver (Skt. *śrāmaṇera-saṃvara*).

27 The seven heinous acts are shedding the blood of a buddha, killing one's father or mother, killing a monk or teacher, disrupting the sangha, and killing an arhat.

28 See note 11 for the eight difficulties.

29 A thousand *li* is approximately three hundred and fifty miles.

30 *Danqi* is an ancient Chinese wooden board game using small pieces; players compete to flick their pieces the greatest distance.

31 Skt. *kuśa-vandhana*. In ancient India a monk was mugged by a thief, who restrained him by tying him up in tall live grass. The monk, not wanting to break the precept against taking life, remained lying tied up in the grass rather than ripping it out. A king who passed by and found the monk was so moved by this scene that he converted to Buddhism. This story is originally told in the *Kalpanā maṇḍitikā* (T.201.4:268c10) and is repeated in many East Asian Buddhist texts.

32 See Fazang, T.1813.40:653a1.

33 In one of Śākyamuni's previous incarnations he is said to have written a certain *gāthā* (four-line verse) containing the essence of the Dharma on a piece of his own flayed skin, using one of his own bones split into the shape of a pen and for ink his own blood.

34 This inline note is found in Uijeok's commentary, *Bosal gyebon so* (T.1814.40:688a21–23), as part of the main text of the sutra but it is in neither the Taishō edition nor the *Hanguk bulgyo jeonseo* (*Collected Works of Korean Buddhism*). It is not clear from his commentary whether Fazang had this text available to him. This precept certainly makes much more sense with the additional text.

Glossary

afflictions (Skt. *kleśa*): Affective disorders, defilement(s); mental disturbances; emotional negativity. All of the thoughts, words, actions, and emotions that arise and cease based on nescience and desire that keep human beings trapped in the cycle of birth and death, and which result in suffering. Buddhism teaches methods for attaining nirvana/enlightenment as a means of eliminating the afflictions.

bodhi: Awakening; enlightenment.

bodhicitta: The awakened mind; the mind that perceives the real behind the seeming, believes in moral consequences, and that all sentient beings possess buddha-nature, and which aims at buddhahood. The aspiration to realize *bodhi*-wisdom, i.e., perfect enlightenment.

bodhisattva: A Buddhist practitioner intent on the attainment of enlightenment based on profoundly altruistic motivations (*bodhicitta*). The model practitioner in the Mahayana tradition, a bodhisattva dedicates his or her efforts to the salvation of other beings. This concept is used in Mahayana texts to distinguish from the earlier Indian spiritual ideal of the arhat, who also attains a form of enlightenment but whose realization is considered to be inferior due to the individual orientation of the practices pursued in its attainment. *See also bodhicitta;* Mahayana.

brahmā: A god (Skt. *deva*) regarded as the creator of the universe in the Vedic tradition, but relegated to a lesser role in Buddhism; capitalized, it is the proper name for the king of the *deva*s, as well as a descriptive term for a group of higher celestial *deva*s.

buddha-nature: The innate buddha-mind, indicating the potential to actualize buddhahood, possessed by sentient beings. Buddha-nature is understood as being not fully actualized prior to the full attainment of buddhahood; thus sentient beings are required to purify themselves through practice to achieve its realization.

dependent arising (Skt. *pratītyasamutpāda*): The fundamental Buddhist teaching that all things arise due to particular conditions; nothing arises out of nothing and nothing arises of itself; things do not come into existence through the power of an external creator. Therefore there is nothing that is self-contained, independent, or that has its own separate and independent nature. Dependent arising is the condition of things arising or being produced only in relationship to their causes and conditions.

Dharma: The term has a wide range of meanings in Buddhism but its foremost meaning is the teaching delivered by the Buddha that is fully accordant with reality, and connotes Buddhism as the perfect religion; truth, reality, true principle, law. It is also used as a common noun (lower-case), in the sense of "all things," anything small or great, visible or invisible, real or unreal, affairs, truth, principle, method, concrete things, abstract ideas, etc.

dharmakāya ("Dharma body"): Translated as reality body, truth body, etc. In general Mahayana teaching the Dharma body is a name for absolute existence, the manifestation of all existences; the true body of reality, or the Buddha as eternal principle; the body of essence that is pure, possesses no marks of distinction, and is the same as emptiness. One of the three bodies of a buddha. *See also* three bodies.

dhūta: Austerities. The original Indic term means literally "to cast off," shake off, cleanse, etc. Used in this text, it indicates casting off afflicted attachments through ascetic practices designed to eliminate the practitioner's attachment to food, clothing, shelter, etc. There are twelve categories of *dhūta* practices.

Four-part Vinaya (Skt. **Dharmaguptaka-vinaya;* Ch. *Sifen lu;* T. 1428): An influential vinaya (collection of monastic codes) text transmitted from the Dharmaguptaka school, translated by Buddhayaśas (408–413 C.E.) and Fonian (412–413 C.E.). One of four major Indian vinaya works transmitted to East Asia, it remained popular among monastics after the appearance of the *Brahmā's Net Sutra. See also* Vinaya.

Flower Ornament Sutra (Skt. *Avataṃsaka-sūtra;* Ch. *Huayan jing*): One of the most influential sutras in East Asian Buddhism, of which three Chinese translations, all entitled *Dafangguang fo huayan jing,* were made. The text describes a cosmos of infinite realms that mutually contain and interpenetrate each other. The vision expressed in this work was the foundation for the creation of the Huayan school of Buddhism, which was characterized by a philosophy of interpenetration.

four groups of practitioners (*catuṣpariṣad*): The four categories of Buddhist followers, consisting of monks, nuns, laymen, and laywomen.

humaneness (*ren*): Consideration for others; altruism; goodness, kindness, compassion, benevolence. In the thought of Confucius and Mencius, it is the basic quality of unselfishness contained to one degree or another in the minds of all human beings, which is the basis for the appearance of all proper forms of human interaction such as justice, filial piety, trustworthiness, propriety, and so forth.

Hinayana ("Lesser Vehicle"): As opposed to the term Mahayana ("Great Vehicle"), the term refers in general to Buddhist practices centered on individual salvation, which are not based on the true experience of emptiness. Used in a historical interpretive sense, Hinayana refers to the early Indian groups typified by Theravādins and Sarvāstivādins that held to a monastically centered approach to Buddhist practice. In Mahayana texts, the Hinayana practices of *śrāvaka*s (disciples) and *pratyekabuddha*s (self-enlightened ones) are held to be flawed in that they lack the penetrating view of emptiness and the universally functioning compassion possessed by bodhisattvas in the Mahayana path. *See also* Mahayana; *pratyekabuddha; śrāvaka.*

kalpa: An eon, a world-period; in Indian cosmology, the longest period of time; an age consisting of the span of time between the creation, destruction, and recreation of a world or universe.

Kumārajīva (344–413 C.E.): A renowned translator of Indian Buddhist texts into Chinese. He was born into a noble family of Kucha; his father was Indian and his mother was a princess of Karashahr. Kumārajīva was well learned in Mahayana Buddhism but developed a special interest in the Madhyamaka doctrine of Nāgārjuna. In 401 he was brought to the capital of Chang'an by the ruler Fujian, and with the aid of numerous collaborators and assistants he became one of the most prolific translators of Buddhist texts in history, rendering some seventy-two texts into Chinese. The translation of the *Brahmā's Net Sutra* is apocryphally attributed to Kumārajīva. *See also* Madhyamaka; Mahayana; Nāgārjuna.

liang: An ancient Chinese unit of weight, which varied between fourteen and thirty-eight grams during different historical periods.

Madhyamaka: One of the major streams of Indian Mahayana Buddhism, which exerted a profound impact on all subsequent forms of Buddhism that arose in East Asia and Tibet. Based chiefly in the "middle way" philosophy of Nāgārjuna, Mādhyamika thinkers sought to investigate a middle ground between the two extremes of existence and nonexistence of things. The Mādhyamaka claims that the dependent arising of all things amounts to their lack of, or being "empty of," any independent essence. *See also* Nāgārjuna.

Mahayana ("Great Vehicle"): The name of a late Indian sectarian movement that became the main form of Buddhism in East Asia. The term was created along with and in opposition to the disparaging term Hinayana, used by the former to distinguish the two. In the polemical sense, the concept of a "great vehicle" refers to the fact that the Mahayana considered their doctrines to be more open and universal, advocating that enlightenment was attainable by all sentient beings, including lay followers and householders, rather than only available to monastics who practiced in the pure environment of a monastery. This movement produced a large body of new sutras, in which its new model practitioner, the bodhisattva, preached the doctrine of the emptiness of all things. *See also* bodhisattva; Hinayana.

Nāgārjuna (second–third centuries C.E.): One of the most esteemed figures in Buddhist history, considered by many Mahayanists as second in insight and importance only to the Buddha himself. He was a master of Sanskrit grammar and linguistics as well as a devastating debater and critical thinker, and his masterwork, the *Mūlamadhya-maka-kārikā* (*Fundamental Verses on the Middle Way*), sharply critiqued with elegant, sophisticated verse many treasured concepts and theories held by Buddhists and non-Buddhists, from causality and time to karma and nirvana. *See also* Madhyamaka; Mahayana.

nescience (Skt. *avidyā*): Ignorance, delusion, folly. The fundamental misunderstanding of reality that underlies all the suffering of unenlightened people; the first of the twelve links of dependent arising. Nescience is not the mere lack of factual knowledge but a basic error in one's mode of perception that prevents people from seeing things as they really are; for example, being unaware of the fact that all things are ultimately impermanent or that there is in reality no such thing as an inherent self. *See also* dependent arising.

pārājika: Grave offenses or transgressions of the precepts; the original connotation of the Sanskrit word is thought to mean something like "overcome by another"; thus, to engage in unwholesome acts while overcome by affliction. The commission of *pārājika* offenses are grounds for the excommunication of a monk or nun (expulsion from the sangha and the loss of clerical status), and a guaranteed fall into hell. Hinayana vinaya texts list four *pārājika*s, known as the four grave offenses. In the *Brahmā's Net Sutra* the consequences of the commission of a "bodhisattva *pārājika* offense" are not so clearly defined, so the term is used mainly to indicate the extreme severity of the ramifications of any transgression of the ten grave precepts.

poṣadha: A precepts meeting that occurs six days each month, on the eighth, fourteenth, fifteenth, twenty-third, twenty-ninth, and thirtieth days, according to the lunar calendar. During a *poṣadha* gathering the *Prātimokṣa-sūtra* is recited, monastics confess their transgressions, and laypeople take vows to follow a set of either eight or ten precepts. *See also Prātimokṣa.*

Prātimokṣa: Literally, "liberation from all afflictions"; a code of Vinaya precepts. In the traditional Indian vinaya texts it refers to the sets of precepts to be upheld by monks and nuns, specifically, a set of two hundred and twenty-seven disciplinary rules for monks and three hundred and forty-eight for nuns, which is recited at every *poṣadha* ceremony, during which all monastics must confess any violation of the precepts. In China, the *Prātimokṣa* text used most often was that associated with the *Four-part Vinaya*. Over time, however, there were efforts in China to replace the "Hinayana" *Prātimokṣa* with a "Mahayana" version that could be used in rites of confession, which resulted in the development of the ten grave precepts, a specific set of bodhisattva precepts as given in the *Brahmā's Net Sutra. See also Four-part Vinaya; poṣadha;* Vinaya.

pratyekabuddha: Solitary realizer, self-enlightened one, individual illuminate, etc. One who lives apart from others and attains enlightenment through direct realization of dependent arising, and who does not teach others,. Along with *śrāvaka*s, one of the two "lower" vehicles of the Hinayana, in contrast to the altruistic ideal of the bodhisattva. *See also* bodhisattva; Hinayana; *śrāvaka.*

samādhi: A state of deep meditative concentration or absorption. One of the three basic elements of Buddhist practice, together with morality (*sīla*) and wisdom (*prajñā*). *See also sīla.*

seven heinous acts: Shedding a Buddha's blood, killing one's father or mother, killing a monk or teacher, disrupting the sangha, or killing an arhat.

sīla: Morality, moral conduct; one of the three pillars of Buddhist practice, together with meditation (*samādhi*) and wisdom (*prajñā*).

six destinies: Six levels of rebirth in samsara undergone by sentient beings in accord with their good or evil actions carried out in previous lifetimes. They are the realms of (1) hell (Skt. *naraka-gati*), (2) of hungry ghosts (*preta-gati*), (3) of animals (*tiryagyoni-gati*), (4) of angry titans (*asura-gati*), (5) of human beings (*manuṣya-gati*), and (6) of gods (*deva-gati*).

śrāvaka ("voice-hearer"): Originally, a direct disciple of the Buddha, one who heard him teach; the term later came to refer generally to a Buddhist disciple. In Mahayana texts it is used as a technical term with somewhat negative connotations. While *śrā-vaka*s are disciplined monk-practitioners who contemplate the principle of the fundamental Buddhist teaching of the Four Noble Truths in order to attain arhatship, and thus eventually nirvana, they are also considered, along with *pratyekabuddha*s, to be followers of the two "lower" vehicles, inferior in insight and compassion to the Mahayana path of the bodhisattva. *See also* bodhisattva; Mahayana; *pratyeka-buddha;* two vehicles.

ten unwholesome activities (Skt. *daśâkuśala-karma-patha*): Ten unwholesome activities carried out through the three modes of action of body, speech, and mind (thought): (1) killing, (2) stealing, (3) engaging in debauchery, (4) lying, (5) flattery, (6) insulting speech, (7) treachery, (8) covetousness, (9) anger, and (10) holding false views.

three bodies (Skt. *trikāya*): The three bodies of a buddha, consisting of *dharmakāya, saṃbhogakāya,* and *nirmāṇakāya.* The *dharmakāya* refers to the transcendence of form and realization of true thusness. The *saṃbhogakāya* is the "reward body" or "body of enjoyment" of a buddha resulting from merits attained as a bodhisattva. The *nirmāṇakāya,* "transformation body," is manifested by a buddha in response to the need to teach sentient beings, such as the historical buddha, Śākyamuni. *See also dharmakāya.*

three poisons: The three basic afflictions from which all other afflictive states ultimately derive: (1) greed, desire, or craving (Skt. *rāga*); (2) anger, ill-will, or hatred (*dveṣa*); and (3) nescience, delusion, or folly (*moha*). *See also* afflictions; nescience.

three realms: Three realms of existence into which living beings transmigrate, consisting of the realms of desire (*kāmadhātu*), form (*rūpadhātu*), and formlessness (*ārūpya-dhātu*).

two vehicles: The vehicles of *śrāvaka*s and *pratyekabuddha*s, usually cast in a negative light by Mahayanists as representative of the so-called Hinayana, in contradistinction to the Mahayana ideal of the bodhisattva. Followers of the two vehicles are understood as those whose views of practice and enlightenment will lead them to individual salvation, arhatship but not buddhahood. *See also* bodhisattva; buddhahood; Hinayana; Mahayana; *śrāvaka; pratyekabuddha.*

Vinaya: The corpus of Buddhist monastic rules. Along with the scriptures (Sutra), and philosophical treatises (*śāstra*s, or Abhidharma), the Vinaya forms one of the three major components of the Buddhist canon, the Tripiṭaka ("three baskets").

Vairocana ("Luminous One"): A buddha who represents Buddhism's most profound speculation on the emptiness and interpenetration of all elements in the universe (Skt. *dharmadhātu*). Originally the name referred to the light of the sun but later took on the connotation of the buddha as the fundamental principle of the universe. The chief deity of the five buddhas depicted in the Vajradhātu and Garbhadhātu Maṇḍalas of Tantric Buddhism. As the true buddha body, Vairocana is generally recognized as the spiritual or essential body of truth (*dharmakāya*), manifesting as all-pervasive light. He dwells quiescent in the formless realm (*arūpyadhātu*) and is the essence of *bodhi*-wisdom and absolute purity. Also referred to in this text as Rocana. *See also dharmakāya;* three realms.

Bibliography

Funayama, Tōru. "Bonmōkyō no shohon no ni keitō," *Toho gakuho Kyoto Daigaku Jinbun kagaku kenkyūsho* 80 (2010): 178–211.

—. "Bonmōkyō geken sengyo no sai kentō," in Kunio Mugitani, ed., *Sankyō kōshō ron zokuhen,* pp. 127–156. Kyoto: Kyōto Daigaku Jinbun Kagaku Kenkyūjo, 2011.

Gim Yeongmi. *Silla bulgyo sasang sa yeon-gu.* Seoul: Minjoksa, 1994.

Groner, Paul. "The *Fang-wang ching* and Monastic Discipline in Japanese Tendai: A Study of Annen's *Futsū jubosatsukai koshaku,"* in Robert E. Buswell, Jr., ed., *Chinese Buddhist Apocrypha,* pp. 251–290. Honolulu: University of Hawai'i Press, 1990.

—. "Tradition and Innovation: Eison's Self-Ordinations and the Establishment of New Orders of Buddhist Practitioners," in William M. Bodiford, ed., *Going Forth: Visions of Buddhist Vinaya. Essays Presented in Honor of Professor Stanley Weinstein,* pp. 210–235. Honolulu: University of Hawai'i Press, 2005.

Gwon Sangno. *Joseon bulgyo yaksa.* Seoul: Sinmungwan, 1917.

Hui, Seng. *The Buddha Speaks the Brahmā Net Sutra: The Ten Major and Forty-eight Minor Bodhisattva Precepts.* Talmadge, CA: Buddhist Text Translation Society, 1981.

I Neunghwa. *Joseon bulgyo tongsa.* Seoul: Gyeonghui, 1918.

Jo Myeonggi. *Silla bulgyo ui inyeom gwa yeoksa.* Seoul: Sin Taeyangsa, 1962.

Muller, A. Charles. *The Collected Works of Korean Buddhism, Volume XI: Exposition of the Sutra of Brahmā's Net.* Seoul: Compilation Committee of Korean Buddhist Thought, Jogye Order of Korean Buddhism, 2012.

Ono, Hōdō. *Daijō kaikyō no kenkyū.* Tokyo: Sankibō shorin, 1954.

Satō, Tatsugen. "Zen no kairitsu kan to gokai ni tsuite," *Indogaku bukkyōgaku kenkyū* 9–1 (1957): 231–234.

Yamabe, Nobuyoshi. "Visionary Repentance and Visionary Ordination in the Brahmā Net Sūtra," in William M. Bodiford, ed., *Going Forth: Visions of Buddhist Vinaya. Essays Presented in Honor of Professor Stanley Weinstein,* pp. 17–39. Honolulu: University of Hawai'i Press, 2005.

Bibliography

U Jeongsang and Gim Yeongtae. "Silla tong-ilgi hakseung ui jeosul iram, Taehyeon jo," *Hanguk bulgyo sa.* Seoul: Sinheung, 1968.

Yi Mang. *Silla Taehyeon ui yusik sasang yeon-gu.* Seoul: Dongjjok nara, 1989.

Index

A

Abhidharma, 58
ācārya, 48, 79n23
accusations, precept against, 52
actions/deeds, speech, and thought, 30, 36
    See also body, speech, and mind
administrative duties, precept against
    improper fulfillment of, 58
aggregate(s), 16, 17, 20
    of bodily form, 23
    five, 8, 12
Ākāśagarbha, 36
alcohol, xx, 45
    drinking, precept against, 48–49
    selling, precept against, 45
animals, 43, 44, 45, 55, 59, 70, 71, 78n11
    badgers, 62
    captive, releasing, 55
    cats, 62
    cattle, 71
    dogs, 62
    horse(s), 37, 71
    raising, precept against, 62
    sheep, 71
    six kinds of, 52
    swine, 62, 71
auspicious sign/vision, 57, 69
austerities, 65

B

Beommanggyeong bosal gyebon sagi, xviii
Beommanggyeong gojeokgi, xviii

Bhagavan, 76
    See also Buddha
bhikṣu, xix, 43, 45, 47, 72, 73, 80n26
    See also monk(s)
bhikṣuṇī, 43, 45, 47, 73, 80n26
    See also nun(s)
bodhi, 4, 11, 75
    -mind, 21
bodhicitta. See bodhi, -mind; enlighten-
    ment, aspiration/determination/
    intention for, mind of
bodhisattva(s), xvii, 4–8, 12, 21, 25, 36,
    38, 40–49, 50, 51–55, 61, 63, 65,
    66, 68–74, 75, 76, 77n6, 78n7
    beginner/newly initiated, 41, 53, 56, 57, .
    67
    Dharma teacher/preceptor, 68
    future, 43, 73
    householder/lay, 45, 59
    image(s), 57, 61, 65, 69
    mind-ground(s), ten, xviii, 6
    monk(s)/renunciant, 45, 53, 56, 58, 59,
    65, 72
    past, 43, 73, 75
    path, 5, 58
    practice(s), 4, 54
    precepts, xviii, xx, 3, 4, 41–42, 43, 48,
    54, 57, 69, 73, 74, 79n19
Bodhisattva Prātimokṣa, xviii
    *See also Brahmā's Net Sutra; Prāti-
    mokṣa*
Bodhisattva Vinaya Sutra, xviii, 55
    See also Brahmā's Net Sutra; vinaya(s)/
    Vinaya

BDK English Tripiṭaka
(First Series)

Abbreviations

Ch.:   Chinese
Skt.:   Sanskrit
Jp.:   Japanese
Eng.:   Published title

Title	Taishō No.

Ch. Chang ahan jing (長阿含經)   1
Skt. Dīrghāgama
Eng. *The Canonical Book of the Buddha's Lengthy Discourses*
     (Volume I, 2015)
     The Canonical Book of the Buddha's Lengthy Discourses
     (Volume II, 2017)

Ch. Zhong ahan jing (中阿含經)   26
Skt. Madhyamāgama
Eng. *The Madhyama Āgama (Middle-length Discourses)*
     (Volume I, 2013)

Ch. Dasheng bensheng xindi guan jing (大乘本生心地觀經)   159

Ch. Fo suoxing zan (佛所行讚)   192
Skt. Buddhacarita
Eng. *Buddhacarita: In Praise of Buddha's Acts* (2009)

Ch. Zabao zang jing (雜寶藏經)   203
Eng. *The Storehouse of Sundry Valuables* (1994)

Ch. Faju piyu jing (法句譬喩經)   211
Eng. *The Scriptural Text: Verses of the Doctrine, with Parables* (1999)

Ch. Xiaopin banruo boluomi jing (小品般若波羅蜜經)   227
Skt. Aṣṭasāhasrikā-prajñāpāramitā-sūtra

Title	Taishō No.
Ch. Jingang banruo boluomi jing (金剛般若波羅蜜經)	235
Skt. Vajracchedikā-prajñāpāramitā-sūtra	
Ch. Daluo jingang bukong zhenshi sanmoye jing	243
(大樂金剛不空眞實三麼耶經)	
Skt. Adhyardhaśatikā-prajñāpāramitā-sutra	
Eng. *The Sutra of the Vow of Fulfilling the Great Perpetual Enjoyment and Benefiting All Sentient Beings Without Exception* (in *Esoteric Texts,* 2015)	
Ch. Renwang banruo boluomi jing (仁王般若波羅蜜經)	245
Skt. *Kāruṇikārājā-prajñāpāramitā-sutra	
Ch. Banruo boluomiduo xin jing (般若波羅蜜多心經)	251
Skt. Prajñāpāramitāhṛdaya-sutra	
Ch. Miaofa lianhua jing (妙法蓮華經)	262
Skt. Saddharmapuṇḍarīka-sutra	
Eng. *The Lotus Sutra* (Revised Second Edition, 2007)	
Ch. Wuliangyi jing (無量義經)	276
Eng. *The Infinite Meanings Sutra* (in *Tiantai Lotus Texts,* 2013)	
Ch. Guan Puxian pusa xingfa jing (觀普賢菩薩行法經)	277
Eng. *The Sutra Expounded by the Buddha on Practice of the Way through Contemplation of the Bodhisattva All-embracing Goodness* (in *Tiantai Lotus Texts,* 2013)	
Ch. Dafangguang fo huayan jing (大方廣佛華嚴經)	279
Skt. Avataṃsaka-sutra	
Ch. Shengman shizihou yisheng defang bianfang guang jing	353
(勝鬘師子吼一乘大方便方廣經)	
Skt. Śrīmālādevīsiṃhanāda-sutra	
Eng. *The Sutra of Queen Śrīmālā of the Lion's Roar* (2004)	
Ch. Wuliangshou jing (無量壽經)	360
Skt. Sukhāvatīvyūha	
Eng. *The Larger Sutra on Amitāyus* (in *The Three Pure Land Sutras,* Revised Second Edition, 2003)	
Ch. Guan wuliangshou fo jing (觀無量壽佛經)	365
Skt. *Amitāyurdhyāna-sutra	
Eng. *The Sutra on Contemplation of Amitāyus* (in *The Three Pure Land Sutras,* Revised Second Edition, 2003)	

Title	Taishō No.

Ch. Amituo jing (阿彌陀經)　　　　　　　　　　　　　　　　　366
Skt. Sukhāvatīvyūha
Eng. *The Smaller Sutra on Amitāyus* (in *The Three Pure Land Sutras,*
　　Revised Second Edition, 2003)

Ch. Da banniepan jing (大般涅槃經)　　　　　　　　　　　　374
Skt. Mahāparinirvana-sutra
Eng. *The Nirvana Sutra* (Volume I, 2013)

Ch. Fochuibo niepan lüeshuo jiaojie jing (佛垂般涅槃略説教誡經)　　389
Eng. *The Bequeathed Teaching Sutra* (in *Apocryphal Scriptures,* 2005)

Ch. Dizang pusa benyuan jing (地藏菩薩本願經)　　　　　　　412
Skt. *Kṣitigarbhapraṇidhāna-sutra

Ch. Banzhou sanmei jing (般舟三昧經)　　　　　　　　　　　418
Skt. Pratyutpanna-buddhasammukhāvasthita-samādhi-sutra
Eng. *The Pratyutpanna Samādhi Sutra* (1998)

Ch. Yaoshi liuli guang rulai benyuan gongde jing　　　　　　　450
　　(藥師琉璃光如來本願功德經)
Skt. Bhaiṣajyaguru-vaiḍūrya-prabhāsa-pūrvapraṇidhāna-viśeṣavistara

Ch. Mile xiasheng chengfo jing (彌勒下生成佛經)　　　　　　454
Skt. *Maitreyavyākaraṇa
Eng. *The Sutra that Expounds the Descent of Maitreya Buddha
　　and His Enlightenment* (2016)

Ch. Wenshushili wen jing (文殊師利問經)　　　　　　　　　468
Skt. *Mañjuśrīparipṛcchā
Eng. *The Sutra of Mañjuśrī's Questions* (2016)

Ch. Weimojie suoshuo jing (維摩詰所説經)　　　　　　　　　475
Skt. Vimalakīrtinirdeśa-sutra
Eng. *The Vimalakīrti Sutra* (2004)

Ch. Yueshangnü jing (月上女經)　　　　　　　　　　　　　480
Skt. Candrottarādārikā-paripṛcchā

Ch. Zuochan sanmei jing (坐禪三昧經)　　　　　　　　　　　614
Eng. *The Sutra on the Concentration of Sitting Meditation* (2009)

Ch. Damoduoluo chan jing (達磨多羅禪經)　　　　　　　　　618

Ch. Yuedeng sanmei jing (月燈三昧經)　　　　　　　　　　　639
Skt. Samādhirāja-candrapradīpa-sutra

Title	Taishō No.
Ch. Shoulengyan sanmei jing (首楞嚴三昧經) Skt. Śūraṅgamasamādhi-sutra Eng. *The Śūraṅgama Samādhi Sutra* (1998)	642
Ch. Jinguang ming zuishengwang jing (金光明最勝王經) Skt. Suvarṇaprabhāsa-sutra	665
Ch. Dasheng rulengqie jing (大乘入楞伽經) Skt. Laṅkāvatāra-sutra	672
Ch. Jie shenmi jing (解深密經) Skt. Saṃdhinirmocana-sutra Eng. *The Scripture on the Explication of Underlying Meaning* (2000)	676
Ch. Yulanpen jing (盂蘭盆經) Skt. *Ullambana-sutra Eng. *The Ullambana Sutra* (in *Apocryphal Scriptures,* 2005)	685
Ch. Sishierzhang jing (四十二章經) Eng. *The Sutra of Forty-two Sections* (in *Apocryphal Scriptures,* 2005)	784
Ch. Dafangguang yuanjue xiuduoluo liaoyi jing (大方廣圓覺修多羅了義經) Eng. *The Sutra of Perfect Enlightenment* (in *Apocryphal Scriptures,* 2005)	842
Ch. Da Biluzhena chengfo shenbian jiachi jing (大毘盧遮那成佛神變加持經) Skt. Mahāvairocanābhisambodhi-vikurvitādhiṣṭhāna-vaipulyasūtrendra- rājanāma-dharmaparyāya Eng. *The Vairocanābhisaṃbodhi Sutra* (2005)	848
Ch. Jinggangding yiqie rulai zhenshi she dasheng xianzheng dajiao wang jing (金剛頂一切如來眞實攝大乘現證大教王經) Skt. Sarvatathāgata-tattvasaṃgraha-mahāyānā-bhisamaya-mahākalparāja Eng. *The Adamantine Pinnacle Sutra* (in *Two Esoteric Sutras,* 2001)	865
Ch. Suxidi jieluo jing (蘇悉地羯囉經) Skt. Susiddhikara-mahātantra-sādhanopāyika-paṭala Eng. *The Susiddhikara Sutra* (in *Two Esoteric Sutras,* 2001)	893
Ch. Modengqie jing (摩登伽經) Skt. *Mātaṅgī-sutra Eng. *The Mātaṅga Sutra* (in *Esoteric Texts,* 2015)	1300

Title	Taishō No.
Ch. Mohe sengqi lü (摩訶僧祇律) Skt. *Mahāsāṃghika-vinaya	1425
Ch. Sifen lü (四分律) Skt. *Dharmaguptaka-vinaya	1428
Ch. Shanjianlü piposha (善見律毘婆沙) Pāli Samantapāsādikā	1462
Ch. Fanwang jing (梵網經) Skt. *Brahmajāla-sutra Eng. *The Brahmā's Net Sutra* (2017)	1484
Ch. Youposaijie jing (優婆塞戒經) Skt. Upāsakaśīla-sutra Eng. *The Sutra on Upāsaka Precepts* (1994)	1488
Ch. Miaofa lianhua jing youbotishe (妙法蓮華經憂波提舍) Skt. Saddharmapuṇḍarīka-upadeśa Eng. *The Commentary on the Lotus Sutra* (in *Tiantai Lotus Texts,* 2013)	1519
Ch. Shizha biposha lun (十住毘婆沙論) Skt. *Daśabhūmika-vibhāṣā	1521
Ch. Fodijing lun (佛地經論) Skt. *Buddhabhūmisutra-śāstra Eng. *The Interpretation of the Buddha Land* (2002)	1530
Ch. Apidamojushe lun (阿毘達磨俱舍論) Skt. Abhidharmakośa-bhāṣya	1558
Ch. Zhonglun (中論) Skt. Madhyamaka-śāstra	1564
Ch. Yüqie shidilun (瑜伽師地論) Skt. Yogācārabhūmi-śāstra	1579
Ch. Cheng weishi lun (成唯識論) Eng. *Demonstration of Consciousness Only* (in *Three Texts on Consciousness Only,* 1999)	1585
Ch. Weishi sanshilun song (唯識三十論頌) Skt. Triṃśikā Eng. *The Thirty Verses on Consciousness Only* (in *Three Texts on Consciousness Only,* 1999)	1586

Title	Taishō No.

Ch. Weishi ershi lun (唯識二十論)   1590
Skt. Viṃśatikā
Eng. *The Treatise in Twenty Verses on Consciousness Only*
(in *Three Texts on Consciousness Only,* 1999)

Ch. She dasheng lun (攝大乘論)   1593
Skt. Mahāyānasaṃgraha
Eng. *The Summary of the Great Vehicle* (Revised Second Edition, 2003)

Ch. Bian zhongbian lun (辯中邊論)   1600
Skt. Madhyāntavibhāga

Ch. Dasheng zhuangyanjing lun (大乘莊嚴經論)   1604
Skt. Mahāyānasūtrālaṃkāra

Ch. Dasheng chengye lun (大乘成業論)   1609
Skt. Karmasiddhiprakaraṇa

Ch. Jiujing yisheng baoxing lun (究竟一乘寶性論)   1611
Skt. Ratnagotravibhāga-mahāyānottaratantra-śāstra

Ch. Yinming ruzheng li lun (因明入正理論)   1630
Skt. Nyāyapraveśa

Ch. Dasheng ji pusa xue lun (大乘集菩薩學論)   1636
Skt. Śikṣāsamuccaya

Ch. Jingangzhen lun (金剛針論)   1642
Skt. Vajrasūcī

Ch. Zhang suozhi lun (彰所知論)   1645
Eng. *The Treatise on the Elucidation of the Knowable* (2004)

Ch. Putixing jing (菩提行經)   1662
Skt. Bodhicaryāvatāra

Ch. Jingangding yuqie zhongfa anouduoluo sanmiao sanputi xin lun   1665
(金剛頂瑜伽中發阿耨多羅三藐三菩提心論)
Eng. *The Bodhicitta Śāstra* (in *Esoteric Texts,* 2015)

Ch. Dasheng qixin lun (大乘起信論)   1666
Skt. *Mahāyānaśraddhotpāda-śāstra
Eng. *The Awakening of Faith* (2005)

Ch. Shimoheyan lun (釋摩訶衍論)   1668

Title	Taishō No.
Ch. Naxian biqiu jing (那先比丘經) Pāli Milindapañhā	1670
Ch. Banruo boluomiduo xin jing yuzan (般若波羅蜜多心經幽賛) Eng. *A Comprehensive Commentary on the Heart Sutra* (*Prajñāpāramitā-hṛdaya-sutra*) (2001)	1710
Ch. Miaofalianhua jing xuanyi (妙法蓮華經玄義)	1716
Ch. Guan wuliangshou fo jing shu (觀無量壽佛經疏)	1753
Ch. Sanlun xuanyi (三論玄義)	1852
Ch. Dasheng xuan lun (大乘玄論)	1853
Ch. Zhao lun (肇論)	1858
Ch. Huayan yisheng jiaoyi fenqi zhang (華嚴一乘教義分齊章)	1866
Ch. Yuanren lun (原人論)	1886
Ch. Mohe zhiguan (摩訶止觀)	1911
Ch. Xiuxi zhiguan zuochan fayao (修習止觀坐禪法要)	1915
Ch. Tiantai sijiao yi (天台四教儀) Eng. *A Guide to the Tiantai Fourfold Teachings* (in *Tiantai Lotus Texts*, 2013)	1931
Ch. Guoqing bai lu (國清百録)	1934
Ch. Zhenzhou Linji Huizhao chanshi wulu (鎮州臨濟慧照禪師語録) Eng. *The Recorded Sayings of Linji* (in *Three Chan Classics*, 1999)	1985
Ch. Foguo Yuanwu chanshi biyan lu (佛果圜悟禪師碧巖録) Eng. *The Blue Cliff Record* (1998)	2003
Ch. Wumen guan (無門關) Eng. *Wumen's Gate* (in *Three Chan Classics*, 1999)	2005
Ch. Liuzu dashi fabao tan jing (六祖大師法寶壇經) Eng. *The Platform Sutra of the Sixth Patriarch* (2000)	2008
Ch. Xinxin ming (信心銘) Eng. *The Faith-Mind Maxim* (in *Three Chan Classics*, 1999)	2010
Ch. Huangboshan Duanji chanshi chuanxin fayao (黃檗山斷際禪師傳心法要) Eng. *Essentials of the Transmission of Mind* (in *Zen Texts*, 2005)	2012A

Title	Taishō No.
Ch. Yongjia Zhengdao ge (永嘉證道歌)	2014
Ch. Chixiu Baizhang qinggui (勅修百丈清規)	2025
Eng. *The Baizhang Zen Monastic Regulations* (2007)	
Ch. Yibuzonglun lun (異部宗輪論)	2031
Skt. Samayabhedoparacanacakra	
Eng. *The Cycle of the Formation of the Schismatic Doctrines* (2004)	
Ch. Ayuwang jing (阿育王經)	2043
Skt. Aśokāvadāna	
Eng. *The Biographical Scripture of King Aśoka* (1993)	
Ch. Maming pusa zhuan (馬鳴菩薩傳)	2046
Eng. *The Life of Aśvaghoṣa Bodhisattva* (in *Lives of Great Monks and Nuns*, 2002)	
Ch. Longshu pusa zhuan (龍樹菩薩傳)	2047
Eng. *The Life of Nāgārjuna Bodhisattva* (in *Lives of Great Monks and Nuns*, 2002)	
Ch. Posoupandou fashi zhuan (婆藪槃豆法師傳)	2049
Eng. *Biography of Dharma Master Vasubandhu* (in *Lives of Great Monks and Nuns*, 2002)	
Ch. Datang Daciensi Zanzang fashi zhuan (大唐大慈恩寺三藏法師傳)	2053
Eng. *A Biography of the Tripiṭaka Master of the Great Ci'en Monastery of the Great Tang Dynasty* (1995)	
Ch. Gaoseng zhuan (高僧傳)	2059
Ch. Biqiuni zhuan (比丘尼傳)	2063
Eng. *Biographies of Buddhist Nuns* (in *Lives of Great Monks and Nuns*, 2002)	
Ch. Gaoseng Faxian zhuan (高僧法顯傳)	2085
Eng. *The Journey of the Eminent Monk Faxian* (in *Lives of Great Monks and Nuns*, 2002)	
Ch. Datang xiyu ji (大唐西域記)	2087
Eng. *The Great Tang Dynasty Record of the Western Regions* (1996)	
Ch. Youfangjichao: Tangdaheshangdongzheng zhuan (遊方記抄: 唐大和上東征傳)	2089-(7)

Title	Taishō No.
Ch. Hongming ji (弘明集) Eng. *The Collection for the Propagation and Clarification* *of Buddhism* (Volume I, 2015) *The Collection for the Propagation and Clarification* *of Buddhism* (Volume II, 2017)	2102
Ch. Fayuan zhulin (法苑珠林)	2122
Ch. Nanhai jigui neifa zhuan (南海寄歸內法傳) Eng. *Buddhist Monastic Traditions of Southern Asia* (2000)	2125
Ch. Fanyu zaming (梵語雜名)	2135
Jp. Shōmangyō gisho (勝鬘經義疏) Eng. *Prince Shōtoku's Commentary on the Śrīmālā Sutra* (2011)	2185
Jp. Yuimakyō gisho (維摩經義疏) Eng. *The Expository Commentary on the Vimalakīrti Sutra* (2012)	2186
Jp. Hokke gisho (法華義疏)	2187
Jp. Hannya shingyō hiken (般若心經秘鍵)	2203
Jp. Daijō hossō kenjin shō (大乘法相研神章)	2309
Jp. Kanjin kakumu shō (觀心覺夢鈔)	2312
Jp. Risshū kōyō (律宗綱要) Eng. *The Essentials of the Vinaya Tradition* (1995)	2348
Jp. Tendai hokke shūgi shū (天台法華宗義集) Eng. *The Collected Teachings of the Tendai Lotus School* (1995)	2366
Jp. Kenkairon (顯戒論)	2376
Jp. Sange gakushō shiki (山家學生式)	2377
Jp. Hizōhōyaku (秘藏寶鑰) Eng. *The Precious Key to the Secret Treasury* (in *Shingon Texts*, 2004)	2426
Jp. Benkenmitsu nikyō ron (辨顯密二教論) Eng. *On the Differences between the Exoteric and Esoteric* *Teachings* (in *Shingon Texts*, 2004)	2427
Jp. Sokushin jōbutsu gi (即身成佛義) Eng. *The Meaning of Becoming a Buddha in This Very Body* (in *Shingon Texts*, 2004)	2428

Title	Taishō No.
Jp. Shōji jissōgi (聲字實相義)	2429
Eng. *The Meanings of Sound, Sign, and Reality* (in *Shingon Texts*, 2004)	
Jp. Unjigi (吽字義)	2430
Eng. *The Meanings of the Word Hūṃ* (in *Shingon Texts*, 2004)	
Jp. Gorin kuji myōhimitsu shaku (五輪九字明秘密釋)	2514
Eng. *The Illuminating Secret Commentary on the Five Cakras and the Nine Syllables* (in *Shingon Texts*, 2004)	
Jp. Mitsugonin hotsuro sange mon (密嚴院發露懺悔文)	2527
Eng. *The Mitsugonin Confession* (in *Shingon Texts*, 2004)	
Jp. Kōzen gokoku ron (興禪護國論)	2543
Eng. *A Treatise on Letting Zen Flourish to Protect the State* (in *Zen Texts*, 2005)	
Jp. Fukan zazengi (普勧坐禪儀)	2580
Eng. *A Universal Recommendation for True Zazen* (in *Zen Texts*, 2005)	
Jp. Shōbōgenzō (正法眼藏)	2582
Eng. *Shōbōgenzō: The True Dharma-eye Treasury* (Volume I, 2007) *Shōbōgenzō: The True Dharma-eye Treasury* (Volume II, 2008) *Shōbōgenzō: The True Dharma-eye Treasury* (Volume III, 2008) *Shōbōgenzō: The True Dharma-eye Treasury* (Volume IV, 2008)	
Jp. Zazen yōjin ki (坐禪用心記)	2586
Eng. *Advice on the Practice of Zazen* (in *Zen Texts*, 2005)	
Jp. Senchaku hongan nenbutsu shū (選擇本願念佛集)	2608
Eng. *Senchaku Hongan Nembutsu Shū: A Collection of Passages on the Nembutsu Chosen in the Original Vow* (1997)	
Jp. Kenjōdo shinjitsu kyōgyō shōmon rui (顯淨土眞實教行証文類)	2646
Eng. *Kyōgyōshinshō: On Teaching, Practice, Faith, and Enlightenment* (2003)	
Jp. Tannishō (歎異抄)	2661
Eng. *Tannishō: Passages Deploring Deviations of Faith* (1996)	
Jp. Rennyo shōnin ofumi (蓮如上人御文)	2668
Eng. *Rennyo Shōnin Ofumi: The Letters of Rennyo* (1996)	
Jp. Ōjōyōshū (往生要集)	2682

Title	Taishō No.
Jp. Risshō ankoku ron (立正安國論) Eng. *Risshōankokuron or The Treatise on the Establishment of the Orthodox Teaching and the Peace of the Nation (in Two Nichiren Texts, 2003)*	2688
Jp. Kaimokushō (開目抄) Eng. *Kaimokushō or Liberation from Blindness (2000)*	2689
Jp. Kanjin honzon shō (觀心本尊抄) Eng. *Kanjinhonzonshō or The Most Venerable One Revealed by Introspecting Our Minds for the First Time at the Beginning of the Fifth of the Five Five Hundred-year Ages (in Two Nichiren Texts, 2003)*	2692
Ch. Fumu enzhong jing (父母恩重經) Eng. *The Sutra on the Profundity of Filial Love (in Apocryphal Scriptures, 2005)*	2887
Jp. Hasshūkōyō (八宗綱要) Eng. *The Essentials of the Eight Traditions (1994)*	extracanonical
Jp. Sangō shīki (三教指帰)	extracanonical
Jp. Mappō tōmyō ki (末法燈明記) Eng. *The Candle of the Latter Dharma (1994)*	extracanonical
Jp. Jūshichijō kenpō (十七條憲法)	extracanonical